GOD AND A MAN

GOD ══AND A══ MAN

HOW GOD CAN USE ANY MAN
TO MAKE A DIFFERENCE

BY

TIM BROWN

Steward & Wise
MORLEY, MISSOURI

Steward & Wise
CHRISTIAN & INSPIRATIONAL BOOKS

– an imprint of –

Acclaim Press
— *Your Next Great Book* —

P.O. Box 238
Morley, MO 63767
(573) 472-9800
www.acclaimpress.com

Book Design: Frene Melton
Cover Design: DEBUFONTS Design Studio
            (Tara McCarty and Jennifer Melloan)

ISBN: 978-1-948901-82-6 | 1-948901-82-X
Library of Congress Control Number: 2020952784

First Printing 2021
Printed in the United States of America
10 9 8 7 6 5 4 3 2 1

This publication was produced using available information.
The publisher regrets it cannot assume responsibility for errors or omissions.

CONTENTS

DEDICATION

This book is dedicated to the two people that
have stuck with me and loved me when they shouldn't
have—my Savior, Jesus Christ, and my wife, Mylinda.

I also dedicate it to the following:
Ellwood Brown, Sr.
Harvey Story
Ellwood Brown, Jr.
Sharon Brown
Travis Brown
Tyler Brown
Bob Warren

And also, to all those precious ones who call me "Poppa"

Forever honored and grateful!

ACKNOWLEDGMENTS

*Thanks so much to Scott Coffman, Emily Cassetty,
and Bobbie Bryant for taking my thoughts
and helping me put them into words.
This would not have been possible without each of you.*

FOREWORD

Can one man really make a difference?

When I first met Tim Brown, he was my Sunday School teacher at Living Hope Baptist Church in Bowling Green, Kentucky. Early on in our now two decades of friendship, I realized that Tim was a man called by God to share knowledge and wisdom with others, gifts that God has always given him in abundance. Over the past twenty years, I have been blessed to have Tim be one of just a handful of men God has placed in my life to help and encourage me on my own spiritual journey.

Every person needs other people in their life to encourage them and support them through their struggles, but I think that men in particular need other men to share experiences, offer advice and counsel, and consistently point them towards a stronger relationship with God. Tim has proven to be such a man in my life — someone I can always count on for the truth, even when it hurts. He is always eager to help, whether that entails giving Godly council, imparting advice from his life experiences, or simply listening and being a good friend. He has shown me time and time again that if we will simply humble ourselves, turn it over to God, and pray His will be done, God will show us the path He wants us to take.

One spring day many years ago, Tim invited me to go with him to a small town called Hardin, Kentucky. He told me to bring some friends, as he often did. Tim has always recognized the value in including as many people as possible in whatever he felt God was leading him to do. After a beautiful two-hour drive through the Kentucky countryside, we arrived at a farm with a sign by the road naming the place "The Hill". Tim will have more stories from "The Hill" in this book, but at the time I had no idea how much this little farm in western Kentucky would mean to me. Tim and I and the few men I brought along walked through the door and were introduced to a man I would later grow to love dearly. His name was Bob Warren, and he stood over us with his towering 6'5" frame smiling as he shook our hands. We sat at a large, round table and waited, wondering what great truth and insight Bob might have prepared to share with us. We exchanged small talk for a while, then Bob leaned back in his creaky wooden chair and said in his slow Marshall County accent, "Well, you guys have driven a long way. What would you like to talk about?" I am sure my confusion was apparent on my face. I looked at Tim, and he looked back at me. I was puzzled and embarrassed. I had brought a few of my closest friends with me in anticipation of an enlightening and inspiring message. I thought, "What has Tim gotten me into?" Had Bob not prepared for this meeting at all? He didn't have a Bible with him, or even a notebook. Tim winked at me reassuringly and encouraged my friends and I to ask Bob any question we might have in relation to the Bible. We proceeded hesitantly, and I soon realized Tim Brown knew Bob Warren very well and knew exactly what he was getting us into.

Tim had been spending a generous amount of time with Bob recently and knew already what we were about to find out. Bob had completely memorized every word of the New Testament and the vast majority of the Old Testament. He had insightful, scripture-based answers to our every question. Bob would often make points in our conversation then quote the book, chapter and verse, as a point of reference. Every point was reinforced by and rooted in the Bible. I then realized Bob had been discipling my good friend, mentor, and Sunday School teacher, Tim Brown. I felt extremely blessed; my small-town Sunday School teacher was putting in the time to study under a man who knew God and His Word so well that he had most of the Bible memorized. I silently thanked God, as I have many times since, for allowing my friends and I to cross paths with Bob and Tim in His infinite wisdom. That meeting fortified my friendship with Tim and Bob, but also with the men I brought with me. Those friends have continued to shape my life over the years through their individual relationships with Jesus Christ. That spring day in Hardin, we witnessed firsthand together what a truly deep, personal relationship with Christ looked like.

Years after that initial meeting, Tim continued to be discipled by Bob and in turn continued to disciple others and pass along the wisdom God gave him. God soon placed a desire on Tim's heart to build a men's ministry, dedicated to the discipleship of others using the same methods Bob had imparted to him. This ministry would grow into an organization that, through the years, has impacted the lives of countless men from around the globe. Through years of hard work, Tim has assembled the resources and tools needed to encourage men to get a group of other men together and make irreplaceable, life-changing, faith-shifting differences in each other's lives. Tim's organizational skills, task-oriented mindset, and God-given ability to be a motivational leader have made this a success.

Once you finish this book, you will have a better understanding of Tim's vision to share the empowering and freedom-giving love of Jesus with all men, and hopefully you will recognize that it is a mission we should all be working to accomplish. Understanding the principles taught in this book will make you a better man, a better brother, a better husband, a better father, and a better grandfather. These truths, when passed on as intended, will create a ripple effect emanating from your life that will point more people to Jesus and accomplish more work for the Kingdom than you ever thought possible. Once you start on this fascinating journey, I trust you will quickly realize what I and countless other men already have, this is more than a book or a ministry, this is a way of life.

Can one man really make a difference?

With Jesus, absolutely.

–**Steve Cherry**
Child of God
Blessed husband, father, son, brother, and friend

INTRODUCTION

Can one man *really* make a difference?

That may be what we are thinking, but we must ask ourselves where that mindset has come from. Does that kind of skepticism align with the examples God has given us in His Word? Does anything about that sort of doubt sound like faith at all? If not, who have we been listening to?

Could it be that we have been deceived? Is it possible that we have been duped into thinking that one little, ordinary ill-equipped guy could not possibly make a difference in our world? Have we been listening to the wrong voices for so long that we have come to believe that no ordinary man growing up in Small Town, USA, could be used to do extraordinary things for the Kingdom?

Could it be that if we invested some of our precious time studying the lives of a few ordinary men that God really did use to do extraordinary things, we might start hearing truth again? If we turned our faces and attuned our ears to our Father's voice, could we believe anew that one man really can make a difference?

The more we study the examples in Scripture, the more we familiarize ourselves with the heart of the Writer of these ancient stories, the Writer of our present-day stories. Our God is a God of second chances. When we are reminded of that truth, it will seem so much less absurd that God could indeed take the ugliness, scars, and junk in our past and use them for good. When men discover for themselves who God truly is for the first time, they will learn that not only is He neither appalled nor surprised by their sin, He is even able to use the lessons learned in those hard places as a foundation for an amazing future. God wastes nothing. He overlooks nothing. When we put our messes in His hands, we give Him the opportunity to build a life we could have never built on our own.

When we step back and allow God to do the building in our lives, when we hand Him the pen to write our stories, when we find the courage to follow Him as He takes us on the journey He uniquely created us for, we become the men God created us to be. We get a front row seat to see God do extraordinary things in our otherwise ordinary lives.

When I was a kid, I remember watching reruns of the old television show *Dragnet*. One of the main characters was Detective Joe Friday, who was played by Jack Webb. One of the things that Detective Friday became known for was a statement he would make while interviewing suspects and witnesses. As the interviewees would describe what they saw or heard, Detective Friday would reiterate that he was looking for "Just the facts, ma'am."

I believe you have picked up this book for a reason, but I also know you are probably skimming it to see if it is worthy of your time and attention. Before deciding whether to read much further, you may find yourself looking for "just the facts" about whether this simple account of *God and a Man* is one that really can make a difference.

So, CAN one man really make a difference? Based on what I see in the Bible, I believe the answer is a resounding YES!

One of my favorite people in the Bible is Joshua. I can't wait to meet him someday in Heaven. When you read about him, it is obvious he was not like any other man. Joshua looked at the world through a different lens. He had a passion to truly know God in a very intimate way. As a result, the account of Joshua's life leaves no doubt that he was a man who made a difference.

Here are "just the facts" about Joshua:
- He led Israel to victory over the Amalekites. (Exodus 17:13)
- He spied out the land of Canaan. (Numbers 13:8, 16)
- He succeeded Moses. (Deuteronomy 1:38, 31:3, 7-8; 34:9)
- He led Israel into the Promised Land. (Joshua 1)
- He conquered Jericho. (Joshua 6:2-27)
- He also conquered five kings at Gibeon, as detailed below:

So, Joshua marched up from Gilgal with his entire army, including all the best fighting men. The Lord said to Joshua, "Do not be afraid of them; I have given them into your hand. Not one of them will be able to withstand you."

After an all-night march from Gilgal, Joshua took them by surprise. The Lord threw them into confusion before Israel, so Joshua and the Israelites defeated them completely at Gibeon. Israel pursued them along the road going up to Beth Horon and cut them down all the way to Azekah and Makkedah. As they fled before Israel on the road down from Beth Horon to Azekah, the Lord hurled large hailstones down on them, and more of them died from the hail than were killed by the swords of the Israelites.

On the day the Lord gave the Amorites over to Israel, Joshua said to the Lord in the presence of Israel:

"Sun, stand still over Gibeon,
and you, moon, over the Valley of Aijalon."
So the sun stood still,
and the moon stopped,
till the nation avenged itself on its enemies,
as it is written in the Book of Jashar.

The sun stopped in the middle of the sky and delayed going down about a full day. There has never been a day like it before or since, a day when the Lord listened to a human being. Surely the Lord was fighting for Israel![1]

You read that right. Joshua was bold enough to ask God Himself to make the sun stand still so he and his men could finish their battle. And God did just that! He honored such an unfathomable request! It sounds unbelievable; however, Christopher Eames of *The Trumpet* writes:

If this kind of astronomical event happened, it must have been witnessed around the world. While difficult to corroborate, there are various ancient legends of an incredibly long "day" or "night" from numerous cultures. Harry Rimmer briefly summarized some of them: "In the ancient Chinese writings there is a legend of a long day. The Incas of Peru and the Aztecs of Mexico have a like record, and there is a Babylonian and a Persian legend of a day that was miraculously extended. Another section of

China contributes an account of the day that was miraculously prolonged, in the reign of Emperor Yeo.

"Herodotus recounts that the priests of Egypt showed him their temple records, and that there he read a strange account of a day that was twice the natural length."[2]

One man truly made a difference. Actually, it was God working through a man that made a difference. Never underestimate the power of God and a man.

After I meet Joshua in Heaven, I think I want to hang out with Elijah. I am so encouraged by and I love to read about his zeal for obedience as an ordinary guy like me.

Elijah, too, made a huge difference. Here are "just the facts":

- He was a prophet and predicted famine in Israel:

"Elijah was a human being, even as we are. He prayed earnestly that it would not rain, and it did not rain on the land for three and a half years."[3]

- He was fed by ravens. (1 Kings 17:4-6)
- He defeated the prophets of Baal at Carmel, as depicted below:

At the time of sacrifice, the prophet Elijah stepped forward and prayed: "Lord, the God of Abraham, Isaac and Israel, let it be known today that you are God in Israel and that I am your servant and have done all these things at your command. Answer me, Lord, answer me, so these people will know that you, Lord, are God, and that you are turning their hearts back again."

Then the fire of the Lord fell and burned up the sacrifice, the wood, the stones, and the soil, and also licked up the water in the trench.

When all the people saw this, they fell prostrate and cried, "The Lord—he is God! The Lord—he is God!"[4]

Isn't that hard to believe? Elijah had the courage to ask God to keep it from raining and rain stayed away for years. Elijah called down fire from heaven and it came! There is nothing ordinary about all God did with this ordinary man. One man truly made a difference. Actually, it was God working through a man that made a difference. Never underestimate the power of God and a man.

Another ordinary, flawed man turned Biblical hero that I long to meet face to face is Joseph. I am not referring to the Joseph who was married to Mary and raised Jesus. I am talking about the boy in the Old Testament who wore the coat of many colors. He was so despised by his own brothers that they sold him to strangers and pretended he was dead. Joseph found a way to look past the hurts of men to the hope found in the Lord alone. He was wrongly accused and imprisoned before God exalted him from servant to the second most powerful man in Egypt. This ordinary, once hated, convicted man ultimately saved an entire nation from starving to death.

Here are "just the facts" on Joseph:

- He was the favorite son of Jacob. (Genesis 37:3)
- He interpreted dreams of Pharaoh and his servants. (Genesis 40:5-19, 41:1-32)
- Afterwards, Pharaoh put him in charge of all Egypt, so that he was able to do this:

Now Joseph was thirty years old when he stood before Pharaoh, king of Egypt. And Joseph went out from the presence of Pharaoh and went through all the land of Egypt. During the seven years of plenty the land brought forth abundantly. So he gathered all the food of these seven years which occurred in the land of Egypt and placed the food in the cities; he placed in every city the food from its own surrounding fields. Thus Joseph stored up grain in great abundance like the sand of the sea, until he stopped measuring it, for it was beyond measure.

When the seven years of plenty which had been in the land of Egypt came to an end, and the seven years of famine began to come, just as Joseph had said, then there was famine in all the lands, but in all the land of Egypt there was bread. So when all the land of

Egypt was famished, the people cried out to Pharaoh for bread; and Pharaoh said to all the Egyptians, "Go to Joseph; whatever he says to you, you shall do." When the famine was spread over all the face of the earth, then Joseph opened all the storehouses, and sold to the Egyptians; and the famine was severe in the land of Egypt. The people of all the earth came to Egypt to buy grain from Joseph, because the famine was severe in all the earth.[5]

The same man who was sold by his own family was used by God to provide for all the families in the world, INCLUDING his own! When he was shown a way to store up enough food for people all over the world to buy grain, the Lord revealed again that He uses small people for big purposes. To study Joseph's life is to see that he was used to change the course of history for the nation of Israel. One man truly made a difference. Actually, it was Almighty God working through a simple man that made a difference. Never underestimate the power of God and a man.

The examples in scripture are abundant, but we cannot overlook the power found in the story of David. When he comes on the scene, David is a young boy whose own father, Jesse, didn't think much of him. When the prophet Samuel came looking to anoint the next king of Israel, Jesse didn't believe for a moment David should even be considered. The possibility never crossed his mind. Thankfully, for David and for us, the anointing comes from God, not from man. David was indeed chosen and called out when it was his time to shine.

The young boy was sent to the front battle line to check on his bigger, stronger brothers. While there, he heard that a giant was taunting HIS God and wondered why no one was reacting. David could not be still, and he certainly could not hide, simply because he was told he was too small for the job. Although he was small in stature and belittled by men, the passion for the Lord rose up and made David bold enough to stand tall in battle. When he realized the more suitable candidates were not going to defend God after all, David looked down, used what he had in his hands, and stepped into action. The young boy didn't fret and falter because of all He lacked. He trusted God to use the simple tools and tiny courage that David had and make it enough.

Most people love this story because it is the account of a young boy defeating a giant, but I love it for a different reason. I treasure this tale because of what happens *after* David kills the giant:

> *There was no sword in the hand of David. Then David ran and stood over the Philistine and took his sword and drew it out of its sheath and killed him and cut off his head with it. When the Philistines saw that their champion was dead, they fled. And the men of Israel and Judah rose with a shout and pursued the Philistines as far as Gath and the gates of Ekron, so that the wounded Philistines fell on the way from Shaaraim as far as Gath and Ekron. And the people of Israel came back from chasing the Philistines, and they plundered their camp. And David took the head of the Philistine and brought it to Jerusalem, but he put his armor in his tent.*"[6]

The cowards became the conquerors — all because of one man's actions. One man's willingness to choose courage over fear for a few moments impacted the thinking and spurred the confidence of thousands and thousands of men. An immovable force with a seemingly invincible leader was utterly wiped out because of an ordinary boy's willingness to press into what God was prompting him to do. One man truly made a difference. Actually, it was God working through a man that made a difference. Never underestimate the power of God and a man.

All these men came from different places and had different stories. They had one thing in common, however. Each one of these ordinary men made it his goal and passion to pursue God's heart. That is the common thread that set them apart and made them more than conquerors, no matter what battles they found themselves in.

> "For the eyes of the Lord range throughout the earth to strengthen those whose hearts are fully committed to him."[7]

Joshua, Elijah, Joseph, and David had that in common: their hearts were fully committed to God. All these men were regular men that had made innumerable mistakes. Their commitment to

God did not always protect them from failure. None of these men always got it right, but God saw that each one of these men's passions was to pursue His heart.

> *"The Lord does not look at the things people look at. People look at the outward appearance, but the Lord looks at the heart."*[8]

The world sees the outside, but the Lord sees so much more. All throughout history, we find accounts of how God and a man have done things that blow our minds when we try to understand them from our limited perspectives here on earth.

I have often wondered if we were able to go back in time and walk alongside these real men in their real lives, would we find that they doubted themselves occasionally, too? Surely, they didn't feel ten feet tall and bulletproof every day either. Maybe, just maybe, they felt just like we do at times that they were unworthy to be difference makers. To be honest, I feel very strongly that is precisely what we would discover if we were afforded that opportunity. Why? Because they were just ordinary men like you and I. Jesus Christ was the only truly extraordinary, unflawed hero that has ever walked this earth. Every other man was just that — just a man. *Apart from God, we can do nothing.* (John 15:5)

How about now? What about today? What about in our crazy world? Is it still possible? Could God plus nothing be enough? Could God plus nothing be enough to change history? Over the course of my life, I have found myself wondering if God could possibly take a simple man from a small town in Kentucky and use him to make a difference, too. Could God really take a man who has done so much wrong and use him to make a difference for all the right reasons? Could God still be who He says He is? Could God do what He says He can do? Will He accomplish all He promised in my ordinary life for His glory?

On the pages that follow, I'll follow the Lord's lead in sharing the journey this man has been on with God. It is my goal and my passion to pursue God's heart just like the men turned heroes who have gone before me. I'll expose my heart to reveal more about the Father's. If even one man finds the courage to believe that God can do the extraordinary, then this simple sacrifice will be worth it all.

Deciding to make my daily passion to pursue God's heart changed everything. A decision like that is one that should not be made lightly. God always makes good on His word.

"For the eyes of the Lord move to and fro throughout the earth so that He may support those whose heart is completely His." [9]

To "strongly support" means, in my experience, God will work through those who devote their hearts to Him in order to change things. God will make those men (and women) difference makers for The Kingdom. It is no small thing and it is not for the faint of heart. Those are "just the facts."

In the pages of this book, you'll find the journey of God and a man. This is the tale of how history unfolded in the lives of ordinary men whose entire lives were transformed by God Himself. This is the story of how one man learned firsthand that any man can be who God made him to be, if only he will keep his focus on allowing God to live His life *through* him. This account will prove what can happen when *any* man, despite his past, decides to make God the passion of his life. The true treasure of the tale, however, is the way this man comes to discover that God is who He says He is and that God plus nothing equals everything.

–Tim Brown

GOD AND A MAN

HOW GOD CAN USE ANY MAN
TO MAKE A DIFFERENCE

PART ONE

THE BEGINNING

chapter one

CREATING AN IDENTITY UNAWARE

*O*nce upon a time...no, that's not right.

In a far-away galaxy...no, that's not right, either!

The truth is, when I was twenty-five years old the bottom had fallen out of my picture perfect world and I decided to do one of the scariest things in my short life—physically take out my vengeance on another human being.

When your entire identity is wrapped up in what you do, what you have, and who you know, it's very easy for the enemy to get in your mind and take your thoughts to places you never imagined. And here I was, the perfect target. The business empire that I reigned over as president was falling apart around me due the deception and evil intent of one man. "Mr. Business", as I will describe him, had reeled my business partners and me into his evil trap.

After receiving a phone call from my dad, who was one of the partners, that they had been duped by a dishonest bankruptcy trustee, I decided that Mr. Business was going to pay, one way or another. I left my office and went to the storage room in the back of the store and found a pipe wrench that was about the size of a small billy club. I jumped in my vehicle and headed up the road to pay Mr. Business a visit. When I pulled into his long driveway, the same one I had pulled into numerous times to eat with him and his family, my heart was racing. The spirit of vengeance was rushing on me like a tidal wave. In my mind, it couldn't get any worse. My life was over. I had failed. I had ruined other people's lives. It was all because of him. He was going to pay! I didn't care what happened to me.

I jumped out of my vehicle and hurriedly made my way to his front door. The door was about ten feet tall and made from this beautiful wood with hand carved designs framing the perimeter. I took my pipe wrench and started to beat on that door, leaving scars with every knock from my weapon. I was screaming out of control for him to come to the door. I used profanity after profanity as I encouraged him to come and face me. I'm not sure I have ever felt that much rage before, or since.

Then suddenly I saw the curtains move in one of the front windows closest to the front door that I was redecorating with every blow of that pipe wrench. It was him! He was sheepishly watching me in all my rage.

I kept challenging him to come to the door and face me. I could see the fear in his eyes. I think he realized that I was a desperate man and was willing to do something unimaginable. As I kept beating on that door, I heard sirens in the distance and knew that in his fear he had called the police. Eventually some sense of reason came over me, and I made the decision to get back in my vehicle and get out of there.

I drove around for hours replaying what I had done and thinking of what was next. Finally, I quit driving and went back to the store, fully expecting the police to be waiting for me. Apparently, Mr. Business didn't direct the police to come after me, because they were not there, and I never heard anything from them.

Obviously, I am quite embarrassed to admit that story to anybody, much less put in a book for the whole world to know. But as I look back, I see God was right there. He was protecting me. He was writing His story in the midst of my story. If Mr. Business would have come to the door, my life and his life would have been forever changed. My family and his family would have been forever changed.

How did I get to this point? Well, let's start at the beginning....

If you ask me, there is no better place to grow up than in a small town. Sure, there is the misfortune of having limited options for entertainment, dining, sporting events, and the like. This was true in the small town I grew up in as well. Murray, Kentucky is no culinary capital, and it has never been accused of being cutting edge or trendy in any way. The beautiful part of that reality, however, is the simple things, the things that really matter in the end. Instead of existing as strangers lost in the hustle and bustle of big city life, the people in a small town live intertwined in community. Names go with faces, stories go with families, integrity matters, and hard work is valued.

Small towns are also a great place to dream big dreams. With no neon lights to distract a boy, he is free to hope and encouraged to believe there is life beyond what he can see. I am thankful for that.

Growing up in a small town has played a critical role in shaping my personal identity, from childhood on through my early adult years.

Both of my parents were from nearby farming communities even smaller than Murray. My father grew up on a dairy farm, and his family also worked hard to raise other crops, including, but not limited to, tobacco and corn. Money was tight, but that also served to spur my father on to work hard in the fields and in the classroom. He was an excellent student and decided when he was a small child that he wanted to be a veterinarian. He dreamed big in his tiny town and worked hard to see those dreams come to fruition. He graduated as Valedictorian of his high school class, then went on to excel in college, then in veterinary school just as he had hoped he would.

My mother's parents worked in a clothing manufacturing facility throughout her adolescence. They also helped her grandparents with their farming endeavors. This allowed them to live a slightly more privileged life, but they certainly never lived extravagantly, either. Hard work was always central to their success.

My parents met when my mother was still in high school and my father was a freshman in college. Contrary to the plans their parents had for them, my mother and father married very young. With the birth of my older brother impending, they married at the ages of nineteen and fifteen. (As I write this, I'm proud to say they have been married for fifty-eight years. Ideal circumstances are not always required in real life fairy tales.) I was born three years after my brother, and my sister came a short eleven months after that. All the while, my dad was working hard to reach his goals in veterinary school. He worked three jobs, slept just a few hours a night, and graduated with honors.

The drive to succeed propelled my father in the direction of his dreams and kept him persevering throughout his career. In fact, he would now admit that this drive transformed him into a workaholic. My dad was amazing. He built one of the largest privately-owned veterinary practices in the state of Kentucky. Everybody from miles around knew him. To say he was highly regarded in the community is an understatement.

Unbeknownst to him, my father's determination played a key role in my life, too. Following the example my father was living out before me shaped the man I was becoming.

As I recall, my earliest passion to succeed came while I was participating in youth sports. I absolutely loved baseball. I was passionate about it, really. I could play baseball all day, and many times in my pre-teen years, I did just that. Growing up in a small town, we had the freedom to jump on our bicycles and ride a few miles to somebody else's house to play baseball whenever we wanted. We had no concept of the fears children experience today. There was no thought about being unsafe or in danger. It was a great time to be a kid.

There was nothing I wanted more than to be the best baseball player in my town. I would go out in my front yard by myself for hours at a time. In my mind, I would play a real game as I shadow batted and shadow pitched and played the field. I was driven to succeed even when I was the only one aware of my dream. The example set for me had shown me that reaching dreams was possible, that hoping for greater things was worthwhile, and that practice and perseverance paid off.

My hard work and determination, indeed, paid off. When I was nine years old, I was the only boy my age in the community that got picked to play Little League baseball with the older boys. Then the following year, I was picked again to "play up" and do what I wasn't expected to be able to do. To some, it might have just been a little boys' baseball team, but for this guy? Being part of the All-Star team, and being chosen for it ahead of schedule, confirmed in my heart that working hard and dreaming big was worth it. I learned at an early age how wholehearted devotion could be blessed in ways the world would never teach.

Right around that same time, I also started playing Little League football. Much like I had done with baseball, I decided I was going to be the best quarterback in my community. The shadow games in my front yard were not limited to baseball games, but football games during that season as well. In every season, I wanted to be found working hard, dreaming big, and preparing for what was coming next. I wanted to be the best in whatever I was doing. Mediocre was not an option. Apathy was absent in my life. Passion and the pursuit of excellence were the flames beneath my feet.

Beyond my yard, I sought opportunities to sharpen my skills and learn new strategies. I went to as many baseball and football camps as I possibly could. My television was always tuned to game after game. Every free minute I had was spent either studying or practicing the sports I loved. For much of my life, I either had a glove or a ball in my hand.

Make no mistake, though, hard work in real life played a critical role, too. My father taught my brother and me to raise tobacco and required us to do farm work. It was important to him that we learn to make money for ourselves instead of relying on him to give us money. He could certainly provide for us, but he wanted to provide more than things. My father knew it was his responsibility to equip us to be successful men in the tough world in which he had worked hard to make a way for us. We followed his example, and we, too, learned to make a way for ourselves.

That sounds nice, but it certainly doesn't mean I liked it. I hated doing all that work. To be honest, hate might not be a strong enough word for how I felt about those tasks. For that reason, my father was not one of my favorite people for much of my teenage life. My focus and my drive, which I had quietly derived from him, was all about sports instead of work. My brother was quite the opposite. His focus and drive were on work, not play. He was more concerned with making money than chasing dreams.

In the summer of 1977, I was 12 years old and shooting basketball in the driveway of our house, when a cool-looking car pulled up in the driveway. This tall gentleman got out of the car, walked up to me, and introduced himself as Bob Warren.

I immediately recognized the name. He had grown up with my dad. He had been an all-SEC basketball player for Vanderbilt from 1965 to 1968. He was drafted in the fourth round by the Atlanta Hawks of the NBA but chose to play in the old ABA instead. He played eight seasons for seven different teams in the ABA and had just retired the previous year. Bob had then moved back to his hometown of Hardin, Kentucky (population 353 at the time, a little over 600 now), which is where my dad had grown up as well.

After introducing himself, Bob said he was looking for my dad. Being a veterinarian, my dad had a large animal barn down the lane from our house. He was down there working on a horse. Bob went down there for about thirty minutes or so. Then they both came back up to the house talking, and Bob said, "Come shoot some basketball with me." I'm in awe of him, of course, because he's this pro basketball player and I'm a 12-year-old kid.

Then he asked my dad if I would be interested in going with him and some of the youth from his mom and dad's church to Opryland. (This was the old Opryland when it used to be an amusement park, before it became a shopping center.) My dad said, "Sure," so I wound up going with Bob. I spent the night at his parents' house with him. His mom showed me his scrapbooks, and Bob told me all his cool stories about how he'd played against the likes of Dr. J and many others. I went to Opryland with him the next day.

After I came home, I proceeded to tell all my buddies that I had hung out with a former professional basketball player! I didn't see Bob much after that. Honestly, I had basically forgotten about him until one Christmas years later, but that's another story for another chapter.

When I reached high school, I excelled at both the sports in which I had a passion. I became the starting quarterback my sophomore year on a very bad team. I injured my knee halfway through that year and ended up missing the remainder of the season. My junior year would change everything, as we became one of the top offensive teams in the state and fell just short of the state championship game.

In the summer between my junior and senior year, I started to receive interest from several colleges about playing football. That drove me even harder to improve myself in order to play at the collegiate level. Determined to prove to everyone that I was a college quarterback, I became obsessed with anything and everything that would make me better.

My senior year was my best year, as I established school records in every quarterback category and went on to make All-Conference and All-State teams. I was offered opportunities to play at several small colleges but decided to play in my hometown at Murray State University.

However, in the spring before I graduated, there was a change in the head coach position at Murray State, and I was asked to walk on instead of being on scholarship. I decided against that and made the decision to pursue a football career as a walk-on at the University of Mississippi. My EGO, which stands for *Edge God Out*, had become the center of my actions.

So, at eighteen years old, I was fully focused and driven, shaping my individual identity. I know now that my ego guided so many of my thoughts and actions for many years. At the time, however, I was blissfully unaware.

chapter two

MR. & MRS. BROWN

I spent the summer after high school graduation in Houston, Texas. Talk about culture shock! My brother had moved there the previous summer and was working for an oil rig service company. He was making great money and having a lot of fun. I decided that I would go to Houston and make some money to take to school with me. I figured it would also be a great place to work out for football in the Texas summer heat. It turned out that I was correct about both. Except that I spent all the money I made having way too much fun. I wound up asking my parents to wire me money so I could afford to drive home.

At the end of the summer, I went off to the University of Mississippi for my freshman year of college. My plan was to play SEC football; however, I discovered after I got there that I was in over my head.

There were six quarterbacks on the roster when I reported to fall camp. I was number six. I figured out rather quickly why I had only been recruited by small colleges. The caliber of talent and ability that I was around made it very evident that I needed to look for other opportunities. Luckily, I was immediately placed into the non-roster redshirt program. This allowed me to just go to class and work out with the other freshmen that were in this program.

I came home for Christmas break with an exciting, life-changing opportunity. I was contacted by a friend who was taking a job as an assistant coach at Morehead State University in Eastern Kentucky. They were trying to revive the football program, and he asked if I would be interested in transferring. I love football and Kentucky, and I definitely did not love where I was, so I quickly agreed to make that move. My second semester of college was spent at Morehead.

I also decided to ask my girlfriend, Mylinda, to marry me. To be honest, I am not sure why I thought at nineteen years old I was ready to do that, but I came home for Homecoming, and that's just what I did. I knew she would say yes. We had talked about getting married the entire three years we had dated. I think if you would have asked teachers, coaches, and friends about us getting married, they might have doubted it. We were notorious for being sent to the principal's office for fighting as well as being sent to the principal's office for getting caught "making up."

Then I returned to Murray for the summer break. Mylinda got accepted to attend Morehead State University in the Fall. We were so excited to be able to go together this time, but we had no idea how that semester would forever change our lives. We dove head-first into the exciting opportunities college has to offer socially and reveled in the freedom we found of finally being together on our own.

Christmas break again came with an exciting, life-changing opportunity. This one, however, was even more unexpected than the last. After a semester of carefree fun as independent adults, we discovered we were expecting our first child. Far ahead of anyone's schedule, most of all our own, we sat down with our parents and told them that we were going to get married. Then we shared our other big news. We took the next five days to plan our wedding, celebrate Christmas, welcome the new year, and get married.

Mylinda and I were somewhat fearful, but excited at the same time. We had known since we were fourteen and fifteen that we wanted to be together, and naively didn't think much about the challenges that were ahead of us. Neither of us had any focus on our walk with Jesus, either. We really had no thoughts of any obstacles that this new life might have in store for us.

We spent our wedding night at my parents' house. The next morning, we hooked a small U-Haul trailer to my 1982 Oldsmobile Cutlass Supreme and headed out on a six-hour drive back to college as Mr. and Mrs. Brown.

When we arrived back at college, none of the students had returned yet from Christmas break. I dropped by the student housing office with hopes that someone would be working that day. When I entered the building, there was no receptionist working so I proceeded to walk right into the big corner office. I was surprised to see the director of married housing sitting behind his desk. I introduced myself and explained my situation. He was very sympathetic to our newly minted marriage and was generous enough to forego all the paperwork needed to apply for married housing. In fact, he pitched me a ring with a bunch of keys on it and told me to drive out to "The Blue Zoo" and open as many doors as we needed to. The Blue Zoo was the name given to a mobile home park where the university put all the trailers purchased from the government for married housing. All the trailers in the Blue Zoo were blue (naturally) and had been used as barracks at certain military bases around the country. The director said if we could find one decent enough to live in, then we could just go ahead and move in.

I returned to the car with the new Mrs. Brown in it and told her what the married housing director had told me. I could tell she was a little apprehensive about unlocking a few of the doors at the Blue Zoo to find a suitable place for us to set up our first little home.

We headed down University Ave. towards our soon-to-be new address a few miles from campus. After going through what seemed like fifteen or twenty trailers, we found one that we deemed decent enough and unloaded the little U-Haul trailer that held all our earthly belongings. It was far from fancy, but as a young, married couple desperate for our own space as we anticipated the arrival of our first baby, we thought our little blue paradise was grand—never mind the fact that we had to put furniture over holes in the floor to keep the grass from growing through.

In what seemed like a whirlwind, our lives drastically changed. In a matter of a few months, we went from being free-spirited, independent, fun-loving college students to two kids trying to figure out how to function as responsible, married parents-to-be. We grew up in a hurry. I decided to quit playing football and added a few more credit hours to my load with the hopes of graduating as quickly as possible.

I sought employment in the community so I could provide for my family while I continued taking college courses. Despite the unfortunate truth that Mylinda and I were doing nothing to pursue the Lord at the time, we can now see how He was faithfully providing for us. He was watching over us and directing our path as we stumbled onto one of the most loving families we have ever encountered.

The Jones family ran a local men's clothing business. I met them when I went there asking if they possibly could use some help around the store. Whether or not they really needed help at the time, I am still not quite sure, but they took me up on my offer to help. They hired me and started to give me some hours. Before long, they became our family away from family that we desperately needed, living so far from home. The Jones's treated us like we were their flesh and blood. They embraced every aspect of our lives including our spiritual life. Over the next year and a half, the Jones family was there for us at every turn. They loved us and walked with us through the rough terrain that came with gaining our footing in young adulthood, marriage, and parenthood. They modeled a Christian home and marriage and tried to point us to Jesus.

They allowed us into their homes. They trusted us to babysit their children. They taught Mylinda how to cook. They introduced us to their friends and to leaders in the community. They were with Mylinda when she went into labor and I was at work. They trusted me handling the clothing business and all the things related to running it. They cried with us, laughed with us, and were there to help us pick up the pieces when we made mistakes or were upset with each other.

Allowing people like the Jones family to love and invest in us was such an incredibly loving move of God that I couldn't ignore His intentionality there. I wondered for many years why He cared so much for us that He would put people like them in our lives. Now, further down the road with my Father, I believe I know why. The Lord was trying to consistently show me who He was and is and will always be.

In August of 1985, I received the title of "Father" when we welcomed Travis into the world. I did not know what that title actually meant and, unfortunately, wouldn't fully realize it until nearly twenty years later.

After my son was born, I was more focused than ever on finishing my degree as quickly as possible. In the spring of 1986, I was able to work it out with my advisor to complete the last three hours I needed for my degree as co-op hours. A family I worked for while growing up in Murray was opening a new men's retail clothing store in Paducah, Kentucky, and they hired me to work for them there.

Our little family moved into a rental house while I started to work full-time and embarked on what would prove to be one of the worst periods of my life. I became everything I swore I would not be—a worthless husband, a horrible father, and focused entirely on myself. I volunteered to work until closing every night and then would stay a few hours afterward doing things I had no business doing, especially as a husband and a father.

As I look back now, I am so ashamed of who I had become. I was living my life as though I wasn't married and wasn't a father. I was continually abusing the blessings that I had received, and I was blind to the fact that they were blessings at all. I could not see that I was on a path of self-destruction, a path that I had chosen for myself. I would have never dreamed then that God could ever use a guy like me to make a difference. It was simply not on my radar. It would have seemed impossible to me then. Even so, God knew all along that, deep down inside of me, He had planted the ability and the desire to become that man—God's man.

Whenever I think about this particular chapter of my life, I think I know how Paul might have felt when he looked back at his early life and the way he hurt others, especially those that were followers of the new movement of Jesus. I am sure being used by God was the last thing he could imagine happening to him when he was hurting so many and working against the ways of God.

I am confident that our enemy delights in placing those thoughts in our minds that convince us we could never be worthy, that we would be the last ones chosen to achieve good in the world, that we are not fit for the Kingdom or Kingdom work. Satan uses those thoughts as obstacles to prevent us from seeing and believing that God and a man can truly make a difference after all.

If I elaborated in more detail the way I was living my life at this time, you would probably stop reading this book. The intention of this book is to point you to the Lord, not to glorify sin. The most powerful truth I can tell from that chapter is that I am able to look back now and see that God was there. He was working. He was searching. I could not see Him. I did not acknowledge Him, and I certainly did not intend to live for Him. I was willfully blind, but my God was still there waiting patiently on me. He never ceased pursuing me. He adored this prodigal for reasons no man could ever understand.

The patience and grace He lavished upon me is unrivaled in my life. The God of the Universe never decided, "I'm going to give up on this guy. He is too far gone in the ways of the world." He had every right. He is holy. I was the furthest thing from it. By grace alone, my Father continually overlooked my decisions and loved me with a steadfast love because HE knew the cross—His cross—was big enough to cover it all.

Sadly, God would be waiting on me for quite some time, because I was just getting started down my path of destruction.

PART TWO
THE FALL

chapter three

THE FALL BEGINS

I n the midst of my self-centered, self-absorbed lifestyle, I could not see the numerous ways God had been extending opportunities to me to turn around, to learn a new way, to get out, to truly be free. Finally, something happened that got my attention. When I had worked for the clothing store in college, I had befriended the man who was the developer of the shopping center where that store had been located.

Out of the blue one day, I got a phone call from him wanting to know if I would be interested in putting a men's clothing store in a new development they were building. I told him that I would love to do that, but I was only twenty-two years old and could not even imagine coming up with the money to do something like that. He told me there was a way to do it if I was willing. After a few months of negotiating, we moved to Somerset, Kentucky.

The Lord was moving in ways I could never have imagined. The man who owned the shopping center also owned a large amount of stock in a local bank. He got a bank note secured for over $200,000 dollars for a twenty-two-year-old and his twenty-one-year-old wife. I knew better than to even ask how.

That man also connected me with another man, whom I will refer to hereafter as "Mr. Business." Mr. Business had been remarkably successful for many years and had built an amazing enterprise of three high-volume men's and women's specialty clothing operations. He was highly regarded in the industry as a very shrewd businessman who could sniff out great deals. The shopping center developer convinced me that the best approach to immediate success was to feed off Mr. Business's name and identity in that part of Kentucky. So, we developed a franchise agreement that would partner me with Mr. Business's buying power and advertising campaigns.

In September 1986, we opened the doors of our very own retail clothing operation. Despite my best efforts to derail our lives forever, the Lord had been faithful and merciful as He continued to open doors and keep us on the path that He alone had cleared for us.

The business immediately took off. In our first year of business, we exceeded our projections. We were suddenly the talk of the town, as well as the retail clothing business in the state. Here I was at twenty-two years old running a highly successful business and moving more and more into the belief that what I did, what I had, and who I knew was who I was. Also, at the same time, unbeknownst to me, I was being reeled in slowly to an evil plan by the man through whom I had franchised the business.

Mr. Business and I started to spend a lot of time together. We would travel to clothing markets and numerous vendors all over the country. We would eat at the finest restaurants and stay at luxurious hotels. He would tell me over and over how he thought of me as one of his sons, especially since, according to him, neither of his sons had an interest in the business.

But what I didn't know was that he was slowly reeling me in for the kill. And I was easy prey due to my identity being so wrapped up in what I did, what I had, and who I knew. I was blinded to what was really going on. I was successful. I was living big. I was IT compared to every other twenty-two-year-old I knew.

What I didn't know was what we are told in Mark 8:36: *"For what does it profit a man to gain the whole world and forfeit his soul?"*[10] I was spending all my time with a man who had already lost his soul, and I was being reeled into the same way of life. I would wind up paying for it dearly by becoming the way out of an unseen financial mess for Mr. Business.

On Christmas Eve in 1988, my wife went into labor with our second child. Early Christmas morning, we welcomed Tyler into the world. What a life I was living. A beautiful wife, two sons, a successful business, prominence in the community, our own home, nice cars—living big! We showed up at First Baptist Church on the Sundays we needed to be there, but mostly to be seen. My edge God out (EGO) way of living was doing fine. I was Superman in my mind. I could do what I wanted to whom I wanted whenever I wanted.

What I didn't realize was what 1 Peter 5:8 tells us:

"Be sober-minded; be watchful. Your adversary the devil prowls around like a roaring lion, seeking someone to devour." [11]

This adversary was using a man disguised as a successful businessman, combined with my own identity that I had created all the way back in my childhood, as the roaring lion looking to devour me.

Just a few months after the birth of my second son, Mr. Business approached me with a business proposal. He shared that he was ready to step away from the business and semi-retire and that neither of his sons had an interest in taking the business over and carrying it forward. The trap had been set. Now it was time to have the prey step into it.

He asked if I thought I might be able to put a group of investors together to buy him out, then have me move forward as owner/operator of the business, utilizing the franchise model for future growth. Well, you could probably guess what my answer was. Absolutely! Just tell me when and where to sign.

He knew the heart of my identity. He knew I wanted it all. He knew where I found my value. He knew greed and power were my sweet spot. He knew I would do whatever it took to make this deal happen.

I approached two friends in the Somerset community who had told me they would be willing to get involved as silent partners if I ever wanted to expand the business. Immediately they jumped on board and we started to put together the plan and action steps to close the deal.

To my surprise, one other person also wanted to get involved in this business endeavor—my dad. He had recently sold his veterinary practice in my hometown for a large sum of money. He had taken some money up front and was financing the rest of it over a few years' payout. He thought the franchise would be a good place to invest some of his money from the sale, so we formed a partnership.

The negotiations moved quickly. We found a bank that was willing to loan us a very substantial amount of money to buy Mr.

Business out and to create a line of credit to run the business. We thought we had the deal done when Mr. Business came back with a totally different proposal that we should have recognized as shady. However, due to my greed and my misguided trust in Mr. Business, I was able to convince the others it was the best course of action and would be more economically feasible on the front end.

The original plan was to do an asset purchase, which meant that we would just get the business assets with no liabilities. The new purchase agreement was a stock purchase, which cost us less up front and gave us all of the assets, but also all of the liabilities. We would not realize the significance of this until later.

We legalized all the documents, secured our financing with the bank, and closed the deal. I became the president, vice president, and secretary in the new corporation we set up, and we were off and running. The final purchase agreement also included Mr. Business being retained as an employee for five years so that he could serve as the face of the business while slowly transitioning me into that persona.

I embraced my new role as big dog in this multi-million-dollar enterprise and moved my young family to the town where the main store was located. I dug myself deeper into the identity I had created of thinking that what I did, what I had, and who I knew was who I was. We continued to push away thoughts of focusing our lives on Jesus, and I became more and more bulletproof in my own mind.

I had the freedom of walking into our accounting office and telling them I needed X amount of dollars to pay my personal bills and they would write a check. Talk about dangerous! I was traveling to clothing markets and vendors on a frequent basis and was living it up along the way. If it was even possible, I became a worse husband and father than I already was.

I had become Mr. Big Shot. I was doing everything in my power to become successful at things that didn't matter and wouldn't ever really matter. I was entrenched in the fall that Romans 1 describes:

21 For although they knew God, they neither glorified him as God nor gave thanks to him, but their thinking became futile and their foolish hearts were darkened. 22 Although they claimed to be wise, they became fools.

25 They exchanged the truth about God for a lie, and worshiped and served created things rather than the Creator—who is forever praised. Amen.[12]

I had chosen this path and God turned me over to those ways. He gives us all a free will to either choose Him and seek His heart or choose the ways of the world. I had chosen the ways of the world. As a result, I was in the early stages of a free fall and didn't even know it.

chapter four

THE GREATEST THING THAT EVER HAPPENED TO ME

Bob Warren used to always say: "Never take measures to alleviate difficult circumstances until you are certain that you have learned all you need to learn from the situation. When you alleviate problems prematurely, you end up having to repeat the class." At this juncture of my life, I had never heard this truth. As I look back, I wonder how knowing this might have changed the way I dealt with the difficult circumstances that were lurking just around the corner.

We were about five months into this business journey, and suddenly, some strange things started to happen. We started getting phone calls and notices in the mail regarding merchandise invoices and payroll taxes that needed to be paid. What was strange was that we had no records of these liabilities. Initially, we informed these vendors and state agencies that they must be mistaken. Eventually, due to their persistence, we started to investigate their claims. Our accounting folks started to discover that these vendors and state agencies were correct. Not only were their claims valid, but several other vendors and federal agencies started calling with even more claims of money due to them.

The realization that something was very wrong started to set in. I called all the partners together and informed them of what was occurring. We decided it was time to confront Mr. Business about all of this.

His initial response was surprise and denial. Because I trusted him, and thought he surely wouldn't cheat us, I accepted his answer and decided it must be an oversight. But we soon found out we were just reaching the edge of an imminent, dark abyss.

As more and more claims of liabilities started to rush in, we decided it was time to bring in attorneys and bankers for advice. We resolved to not make any more payments to Mr. Business and to revoke our employment agreement with him. We also denied him any access to the stores moving forward. We needed some time to further investigate everything and try to re-create the books of the business to get a handle on what kind of mess we had gotten into.

It was also about this time that I got my first serious contact from the Internal Revenue Service requesting that I come in and meet with them. Obviously when the IRS calls you for a meeting, you show up. I sat down with two IRS agents, and they revealed to me just how much hot water I was personally in. Extremely hot!

I was informed that Mr. Business had not kept his payroll with-holding taxes current for years, and those unpaid balances were accruing interest at a very rapid rate. It also finally hit me why Mr. Business had changed the setup of the purchase of the business. The IRS agents told me that because we did a stock purchase and assumed all the liabilities along with the assets, we assumed all the tax liabilities as well. The real kicker was that because I was now the only corporate officer, I was personally responsible for the liabilities as well. These liabilities were increasing quickly due to the interest and penalties being added. My big shot world was crashing down.

We decided to confront Mr. Business a second time, but as he had done previously, he denied that he had misrepresented the numbers. The decision was made to file a lawsuit to try to get back the money we had paid to him and use it to pay off some of the liabilities. He filed a countersuit, and the legal wrestling proceeded.

In the meantime, we had a business to run. We had to decide our next steps. After a few meetings, we made the decision to cut our losses and get out. It was decided that we would liquidate the business and try to create as much cash as possible to pay back the banks and the taxes.

I went to New York and found a company that specialized in liq-uidating retail clothing businesses. Within a few weeks, they had a plan of action ready for us to move forward. Over the next six months, we ran the liquidation sale and started to pay off secured debt to the banks and make settlement offers to unsecured debtors. While this process was unfolding, we were pursuing our lawsuit with Mr. Business. I was also trying to negotiate with the IRS to settle all the tax liabilities.

Meanwhile, my dad met with an attorney to get some advice on how to handle any shortfall with the banks that we would be personally responsible for after the asset liquidation. This attorney recommended that he file personal bankruptcy individually. My mother would not have to file, since she wasn't on the bank loan, and my dad would be able to keep half of his assets protected.

If you aren't familiar with how bankruptcy laws function, here is a crash course. When you file bankruptcy, you are assigned a trustee to oversee the money and the paying of creditors. This trustee has the right to investigate your bankruptcy estate and all the functions within it.

Well as fate would have it, my dad got assigned a trustee that was a devil in disguise. By law, a bankruptcy trustee gets paid for his efforts before anybody else gets paid within a bankruptcy. This trustee had figured out a way to pad his pockets by manipulating his power. He spent months digging into and questioning every detail of my dad's life and finances.

When the estate finally was released to debtors, the trustee had drained it to a point where little was left. All the financial reward my dad had received from selling his veterinary practice was gone. In other words, he cleaned my dad out. (As it happened, in February 2012, this trustee was found guilty by the Kentucky Supreme Court of misconduct for his handling of bankruptcy estates. Most dishonest people get what's due them at some point.)

My dad would tell you that going through that season dealing with that man was indescribable. My dad would also tell you that going through that pain was one of the greatest things that ever happened to him as it led him to a realization of the things that really matter in life. There is no doubt of that now, but at the time it was awful.

As I watched all this unfold, a dangerous hatred and a spirit of vengeance started to slowly stir in my twenty-four-year-old heart. I finally exploded one afternoon after getting a call from my dad updating me on the latest with the bankruptcy nightmare they were enduring.

I was at the main location of the retail business, only a few miles from where Mr. Business lived in his million-dollar home. I vividly remember hanging up the phone from my dad and screaming out loud with a rage like nothing I had ever felt in my life. Numerous thoughts started racing through my mind. My great world was falling apart around me. The IRS was relentlessly coming after me. The business was being liquidated, and my parents were losing everything they had worked their entire life to have. Enough was enough!

When your entire identity is based around the thought that what you do, what you have, and who you know is who you are, it's very easy for the enemy to get in our minds and cause you to do things you never imagined. And here I was, the perfect target.

I decided that someone needed to pay for all this misfortune. That someone was Mr. Business. I left my office with a pipe wrench as my weapon, jumped in my vehicle, and headed up the road to pay Mr. Business a visit. The spirit of vengeance was rushing on me like a tidal wave. In my mind, it couldn't get any worse. My life was over. I had failed. I had ruined other people's lives. It was all because of him. He was going to pay! I didn't care what happened to me.

I was determined to physically harm Mr. Business. His front door was about ten feet tall and made from this beautiful wood with hand carved designs framing the perimeter. I took my pipe wrench and started to do a little redecorating, leaving scars with every knock from my self- made weapon. I was using a variety of choice profanities as I encouraged him to come and face me. I'm not sure I have ever felt that much rage before, or since.

Then suddenly I saw him as he was sheepishly watching me from a front window. He was witnessing a man filled with rage that was willing to do something drastic.

I kept challenging him to come to the door and face me. I could see the fear in his eyes. I think he realized that I was a desperate man and was willing to do something unimaginable. As I kept beating on that door, I heard sirens in the distance and knew that in his fear he had called the police. Eventually some sense of reason came over me, and I made the decision to get back in my vehicle and get out of there.

I drove around for hours replaying what I had done and thinking of what was next. Finally, I quit driving and went back to the store, fully expecting the police to be waiting for me. Apparently, Mr. Business didn't direct the police to come after me, because they were not there, and I never heard anything from them.

Obviously, I am quite embarrassed to admit that story to anybody, much less put in a book for the whole world to know. But as I look back, I see God was right there. He was protecting me. He was writing His story in the midst of my story. If Mr. Business would have come to the door, my life and his life would have been forever changed. My family and his family would have been forever changed.

I was trying to alleviate the pain in my own way instead of enduring it and learning what God wanted me to learn in the midst of it. I did learn, but it wasn't immediate. It was many years later. The time frame of learning isn't on a clock, especially when it comes to God. As I have studied the lives of David and Paul, that truth has become more evident.

I learned the power of emotions in our lives. I learned the power of the mind, especially when the enemy gets you to doubt who you are and to blame yourself for failures. I know it sounds crazy, but I am thankful for that embarrassing story of failure and how The Lord used it many years later to show who HE is and what HE can do in our lives, even when we are running in the opposite direction.

I have to believe that if we had a chance to talk to David about his incident with Bathsheba, and how he plotted to have her husband killed in battle, he would be embarrassed and ashamed of his actions. But he would also tell you that God used it to teach him so much. When you read the Psalms that David wrote many years later, you can witness that fact in his words, such as:

For I know my transgressions, and my sin is always before me. Against you, you only, have I sinned and done what is evil in your sight; so you are right in your verdict and justified when you judge. Surely I was sinful at birth, sinful from the time my mother conceived me. Yet you desired faithfulness even in the womb; you taught me wisdom in that secret place.

Create in me a pure heart, O God, and renew a steadfast spirit within me. Do not cast me from your presence or take your Holy Spirit from me. Restore to me the joy of your salvation and grant me a willing spirit, to sustain me. Then I will teach transgressors your ways, so that sinners will turn back to you. Deliver me from the guilt of bloodshed, O God, you who are God my

Savior, and my tongue will sing of your righteousness. Open my
lips, Lord, and my mouth will declare your praise.[13]

So here we were finishing up the liquidation of the business. We
had shut down two of the stores and were in the final days before
closing the main location. It became evident that we were going
to come up short in creating enough money to pay back the bank
loans and I still had the tax debt hovering over me. Finally, we
closed the main location and sold off the remaining inventory for
pennies on the dollar to a jobber. It was now time to auction off the
antiques, the store fixtures, and equipment.

On the morning of the public auction, we received yet another
surprise. Mr. Business and his two sons pulled up in a large moving truck and bought most of the antiques and fixtures at a huge
discount and drove off. WOW! We realized then that Mr. Business
was getting ready to open a retail store right under our nose.

We tried to block him from doing that and were told we would
need to file an injunction and another lawsuit. Unfortunately, we
had to make a decision—do we spend our money on legal fees, or
do we apply it to the debt? Obviously, the debt won out. Within
a few months, Mr. Business and his two sons opened a new store
under the same name, and we were left to pay for his deception.

The initial lawsuit we had filed against Mr. Business was not
going to move forward due to our lack of financial resources. We
had finally come to a settlement with the bank, but I opted to
file personal bankruptcy (a decision I now deeply regret!) since
I was young and really didn't have any substantial assets. I still
would have to deal with the IRS situation, since tax debt cannot
be bankrupted.

Then, we decided to move back to Somerset, thinking that our
friends would rally around us and I would try to start some kind of
business with their support. We quickly learned that was far from
the truth. Many people we thought of as our friends walked away
from us, as though our failure might be contagious. Instead, we
became the topic of most of the gossip seekers.

I decided to get out and start a direct selling business where
I would go meet with guys in their office and sell them custom-
made clothing. My hopes were that it would provide a means to

stay afloat and support my family. But the hole we were in was too deep. I couldn't put enough dirt in the hole for us to even stand on.

Eventually it all came tumbling down. Everything self-destructed. One morning my oldest son came excitedly running into our kitchen to tell us that we had a tow truck in our driveway. What he didn't know was that tow truck was there to repossess my car since we had not made our last few payments. Then just a few weeks later, I negotiated with the bank to take back our house since we couldn't make those payments either.

Our life was a living hell. I will never understand why Mylinda and the boys stuck around. We were literally homeless. I had no idea what to do next or how to take care of my family. I had no clue that this was just the beginning of God trying to get my attention and that He was working all around me. Little did I know that I would look back at this time in my story and be able to boldly say that what I was going through was *one of the greatest things that ever happened to me.* You might say, "What? Are you crazy?" I would answer by saying that when I say it was the greatest thing that ever happened to me, I say that because it was the start of my path to His feet and a story that could only be explained in terms of Him.

But this story was just getting started.

chapter five

BROUGHT TO MY KNEES

One of my favorite stories in the Bible is the parable of The Prodigal Son. I like it because it shows how a father will embrace his son regardless of the journey and the mistakes that the son has endured, even when the son has disrespected the father. I also like the part of the parable when the son is brought to his knees in the slop with the swine and realizes his need to return to his father and his willingness to do it despite being unsure of how the father would respond:

> *So he went and hired himself out to one of the citizens of that country, and he sent him into his fields to feed swine. And he would have gladly filled his stomach with the pods that the swine were eating, and no one was giving anything to him.*[14]

There is something so powerful in the imagery of being brought to your knees. It shows a lack of individual strength. It shows an "I've tried everything else" attitude. It sends a message that I give up trying my own ways. I believe the most important lesson in the parable of The Prodigal Son isn't that the father embraced his son and celebrated his return. I believe it is that the son was brought to his knees and realized he had nowhere to turn except to the father.

People that know a little of my story often ask me what my turning point was. I respond by saying, "Being brought to my knees after trying everything else in the world. When the dust settled, the only thing still standing was Jesus, so I decided to pursue Him. He embraced me despite what I had done!"

But wait, I haven't told you about being on my knees in the slop with the swine....

After losing our cars and our home, we decided to move back to Murray and ask our family to help us. We found a small house out in the country that a family friend let us rent. My father-in-law bought us a car so I could keep trying to go out and sell clothes to men in their offices. It was tough. I needed the money from my sales to try and live, but I also needed that money to pay vendors to get the merchandise for my clients. I quickly realized that this was not going to work.

One cold and rainy December morning, the wheels finally came off. Mylinda had taken the boys to her parents' house, and I was alone in the little rental house trying to book some appointments to sell clothes. I noticed a flyer on the kitchen table promoting Christmas shopping, and it had pictures of the hottest new toys. I felt this warm rush come over my body and my emotions exploded. I had two young boys that were expecting something from Santa, and their Santa couldn't begin to buy the first toy. What kind of dad was I? What was I going to do? Then it happened.

As the cold rain started beating harder on the roof and the windows, I got on my knees and crawled into a corner of the living room and begin to cry like I had never done in my entire life. I began to shiver and shake. I began to cry out, "God are you there? Why me? Help me! What do I need to do? What can I do? Help me God!"

I cried for what seemed like hours. I prayed (I guess?) for most of that time. I pleaded for help. I laid prostrate on the floor and begged for mercy. I remember wondering if God was even listening. Why would He? Who was I to Him? I didn't know a lot about the Father, but I felt sure I wasn't much of a son.

I don't know how long I was balled up in that corner but at some point, the tears stopped flowing. My cries for mercy and help ceased. The cold rain quit beating on the roof and windows. A calmness came over me. Then something happened that to this day I can't explain. Out of nowhere came this message in my mind, "Go to the phone and call the Lexington, Kentucky office of The Tom James Clothing Company."

The first thing you need to know is that I knew nobody at that company. I was familiar with it from my days back in Morehead when Mr. Jones, for whom I worked during college, had worked for them for a brief time. That was it. I knew nobody. So, to say that this "message" made no sense to me would be an understatement. But what did I have to lose?

After trying to process what had happened, I picked up the phone, called directory assistance, and got the phone number. I dialed it but hung up before someone answered. *"What am I going to say?,"* I thought. *"That I got a message from God to call your office?"* Yeah, right.

After a few more minutes, I dialed the number again. This time someone answered, but I said nothing and hung up. *"Am I really going to make this random call to ask for a job?"* I thought. Then I came to my senses. "Do I have a better solution to my problems? Nope!"

I dialed the number for a third time and a woman answered the call. "My name is Tim Brown," I said, "and I was wondering if you might be hiring salespeople?" The voice on the other end replied that she was the wife of Ralph Egbert, the sales manager, and that they were always looking for new salespeople. She stated her husband was on another line, but if I left my name and number, he would call me.

I did what she requested, and within the hour, Ralph called me back. I told him I was looking for a sales position, and he asked me to tell him a little about myself. *"Do I have to?"* I thought to myself. *"There is no way he will hire me if I tell him my background. I'm a mess. My life is a mess."* I had no choice though, so I spilled it all to him.

When I finished, he said to me that he was familiar with our lawsuit with Mr. Business. He had seen it in the local newspaper. Then he threw me a curve. He asked me to come up and spend a day with him out in the sales field, so I could see what the job required, and so he could get to know me.

We arranged for me to spend a day with him the following week. Since I couldn't afford a hotel room, I left Murray at 3 AM on the day I was to meet with him. I arrived at his office at 5:30 AM. I was a couple of hours early, so I decided to catch a nap in the parking lot. I was awakened by the sound of car doors closing, and then proceeded to his office. We had a great day together, and I was confident I could do the job and do it well. We finished our day with a phone interview with the company recruiter. I thanked Ralph for the opportunity and drove back home to Murray.

The following day I received a phone call from the recruiter. He informed me that due to my bankruptcy and my pending situation with the IRS, that I fell outside of the company hiring guidelines. But as we continued to talk on the phone, he did something that once again I have no words to explain. He stopped his conversation and asked me a question. "If I hired you, would you do everything possible to make my decision the right decision?" All I knew to say was, "Yes." He then told me he was going to go against company policy, go with his gut, and offer me a job.

He shared with me that he was a Jesus follower, and that he felt the Lord impressing upon him to give me a chance. I then informed him of what had led me to call the company on that rainy cold morning after being brought to my knees balled up in a corner. He then prayed for me over the phone and told me that my start date would be the following week. Wow! Just WOW! I still get chills when I tell that story. When I tell how the Father was writing His story in the midst of my story.

On a cold Monday morning the week before Christmas, I showed up for my first day of training still in awe of how I had gotten to that point. I still had the IRS breathing down my neck. Our finances were still a mess. I was still a mess. Our life was still somewhat of a living hell. But for the first time in my life I had seen some proof that God was real, even though I was a LONG way from pursuing Him.

My Santa Claus dilemma was fixed when I accepted my new job. I was given an advance on my salary, so we could buy some presents for the boys. As we gathered with our family for the typical holiday meal, games, and opening of gifts, Mylinda and I opened a gift addressed to both of us from my parents. Inside the box we unwrapped was a Bible study. This was not a typical gift that we would receive from my parents. As a matter of fact, I asked my mother whether it was actually for Mylinda and I. She informed me that it was and for us to read the letter that was enclosed with the study. Here is an excerpt from that letter:

> *"Because we love you so deeply, we want to share with you the most exciting truth we have ever experienced. This study has opened our eyes to the knowledge of what a walk (life) with Jesus Christ is all about. John 8:32 has truly come alive to us "and you shall know the truth, and the truth shall make you free." For*

years, we could not accept and understand the theology, we had been taught. As the writer of this study says, "it was like trying to put a square peg in a round hole and it didn't fit." But the answers (the truth) are truly there in the Book if we will search. There we will find the "heart of God." I know this is a long study and takes some time. We have never asked much of you, but this we beg of you."

The study was on the book of Romans, chapters 1-8, and was written by none other than Bob Warren. I recognized his name, of course, as the man my dad had grown up with who played professional basketball, shot hoops with me in the driveway when I was 12, and took me to Opryland.

I acted like I was excited about our unusual gift. In reality, deep down inside, the last thing I wanted for Christmas, or any other time, was a Bible study. However, due to the emotion in the letter and my respect for my parents, we decided we would honor their request and start the study.

Little did we know that this would start the most amazing journey and adventure that either of us has ever been a part of. That it would change our marriage. That it would change us as parents. It would change how we viewed the world around us. But mainly it changed how we viewed ourselves and God.

The week after the New Year, I went to the National Sales meeting and met the leadership of the company I had just started working with. I was blown away by the culture that existed there. I returned energized and ready to tackle this new challenge. I was assigned to work in the new Cincinnati/Northern Kentucky office and started my weekly five-hour commute.

We decided to move out of the rental house we had been living in, since I was going to be gone Sunday night through Friday. Since we still had the tax situation, along with other debt, looming over us, we wanted to find a way to not have a lot of living expenses. So Mylinda and the boys moved in with my Granny Brown, who had been widowed for a few years. She had one extra bedroom in her small house, and it became the home for a mom and two young active boys. We crafted a mattress that would slide under the bed. The boys would pull it out each evening and sleep on it while Mylinda slept in the bed. I would be there two evenings each weekend. This was not an ideal scenario; however, it created a lot of memories for my boys with Granny, and Mylinda enjoyed the life wisdom she was receiving.

I was living in a two-bedroom apartment that the company also used as an office. The front two rooms were set up as the office with living quarters being the back two rooms. I settled into my new way of life and attacked my opportunity with vigor and enthusiasm. I hated not being there with the boys during the week, and I regret that I missed so much of that time with them. But this was what I had gotten myself into. Living apart would become our normal for the first two years of my new career.

I became someone who spent a lot of time alone in a car and alone in the evenings at my apartment. I made the decision to use that time to dig into what my mom and dad had so sincerely challenged me to do, "Seek the truth and the truth will set you free." I listened to the cassette tapes from the Romans study over and over as I drove back and forth from Murray to Cincinnati.

I started digging into the Bible as a way of seeking answers to so many of the questions I had. My mind started to be renewed by the Word. It became living and breathing to me. I started to become hungry to know more truth. How had I been so deceived by untruth and the ways of the world?

I also engulfed myself in my career. I was on straight commission and saw that if I put forth the required activity, the results would come. In a sense, I could write my own paycheck. Since the IRS had notified the Tom James Company that they would be garnishing $700 from my check every pay period, I needed to make as much as possible.

After six months of living with my Granny, we were able to rent another home close to Mylinda's parents. At that time, I started coming back to the Murray area and developing some clients, which allowed me to be home for some of the boys' activities. We also started getting involved with a local church that was pastored by a man I had known in high school.

My marriage was growing in ways it never had before. I qualified for a leadership role with the company, and my income was starting to grow. But we still had this IRS cloud hanging over us and would for an estimated ten years if we couldn't get them to settle the debt with us. I met with IRS agents on several occasions, but they would not settle the debt with me due to my young age and the opportunity to make a good income. They were determined to squeeze every dime possible out of me.

As I continued to move up the company leadership ladder, the time came to make another major decision. I could now hire and develop a sales team and get paid a leadership income by running my own office. But to do that effectively, I needed to live in the Cincinnati/Northern Kentucky area. My boss told me that if I would make that move and grow my business to Presidents Club level, and groom someone to take over my office, then I could move to whatever city I wanted and open another office.

I convinced Mylinda to make the move and promised her it would be for two years. I would do my part and grow my business to the point that we could then move back to Western Kentucky and raise the boys for their remaining childhood years.

We found a home to rent in a neighborhood with lots of kids and rejoiced in our new normal life of consistently being together as a family. I was growing as a leader in the company and was flourishing within the people-first culture that was surrounding me daily.

It was during this time that I befriended the Chief Financial Officer of the Tom James Company, who also had a background with the IRS as an auditor. One day he called me out of the blue and asked me if I would mind if he contacted the IRS on my behalf. He was aware of the ongoing garnishing of my paycheck on a monthly basis and wanted to see if he might help resolve the issue. I quickly gave my approval to his request. Within a couple of days, he called me and said, "I need to know if you would be willing to settle this for $25,000 dollars."

My response was, "Absolutely, but I don't have $25,000 dollars." He told me not to worry about the money. He called me back within an hour and said it was done. *WHAT?*

He informed me that the company was sending the IRS a check and that I would have to sign a settlement document, then the black cloud would be gone. He shared with me that the company was loaning me the money at a very minimal interest rate and would take a set amount out of my pay each month to pay back the loan.

I broke down in tears. I was speechless. My mind immediately went back to that December day when I was balled up in a corner and after hours of crying out in desperation, God answered my pleas for help. I thought about how I had been brought to my knees realizing that I could not come up with an answer to my problem. Yet in that moment, the Father was there working. The Father was writing His story in the midst of my story. The Father was loving me in a way that could only be explained in terms of Him.

PART THREE
THE CLIMB

chapter six

A MAN NAMED BOB

For if while we were enemies we were reconciled to God through the death of His Son, much more, having been reconciled, we shall be saved by His life.[15] *(Bob Warren's life verse)*

While I was being a high school football hero in my own mind and creating a false identity for myself back in the late '70s and early '80s, here's what Bob Warren was up to.

After Bob had retired from professional basketball, he came back to his hometown of Hardin, Kentucky, to resume farming. He raised pigs and had some crops, but he lived by faith.

About that time, he felt like the Lord was calling him into some kind of teaching ministry role. So, in 1977 he started a Bible study with college students in this little log cabin he had built himself. He was studying seven or eight hours a day, and he was writing all these Bible studies with the things that the Lord was showing him. His ministry became simply known as "The Hill."

As the Lord continued to increase this ministry, Bob started to expand and put more buildings up on his 220-acre property southwest of Hardin. First, he built the Manna House conference center. Next came The Ark, a dormitory that allowed six to eight individuals to room together. Afterward came a workshop, more log homes for small retreats and sabbaticals, and various facilities for outdoor recreation. By this time, the ministry, now known as B.A.S.I.C. (Brothers and Sisters in Christ) Training, was equipped to meet the needs of all sorts of groups and organizations to gather for studies, retreats, conferences, and camps.

Bob wrote many studies over the years, but he always considered the Romans 1-8 study to be his most foundational teaching. This is the study that my wife and I went through, and it changed our lives.

At that point, Bob became very significant to me again. I was still impressed with who he was, but for a different reason. As a kid, it was because he was a basketball player, but now I saw this man that was different than any man I had ever encountered. He had a peace about him. He had an authority and a confidence in his life I'd never seen before.

We had moved to Bowling Green, Kentucky in 1997, and I had opened my own Tom James office. I was also continuing to work in the Murray area every few weeks. Once when I was down that way, I asked Bob if he'd start spending time with me. He had no reason to. I lived 2 1/2 hours from him. But I asked him, if I drove down to where he was, would he spend time with me? He agreed, and Bob and I started spending days together. Hour after hour, he'd just take me along with him wherever he was going. He was doing all these things with ministry. I would just get in his truck with him and ride around, and he'd teach me principles and truth from the scriptures.

He had also started doing these community-wide Bible studies and invited people to attend. Every Tuesday night at 7:00, hundreds of people would show up on that hill outside of Hardin. I started going to those as much as I could, even though it was 2 1/2 hours away. He saw something in me that I didn't see, apparently. He was the most peaceful, yet passionate man I'd ever seen.

The other thing that started happening about that time was that I began seeing a change in my own father. Dad had been a man that fully believed that what he did was who he was. He was a workaholic. He was a control freak. But suddenly, I started to see these truths of who we are in Christ start to be lived out in my father as well.

One night at a men's retreat, there were about one hundred guys out at Bob's place, and my dad and I happened to be in the audience as well. Bob opened up the floor, and he looked over at my dad, who he'd known his entire life, and he said, "Doc, if you had to say one thing that has really changed your life, one truth that you've learned, what would that be?"

And I heard my own dad, with tears in his eyes, say, "Bob, one of the greatest truths I've ever learned is Hebrews 4:9—there is a Sabbath rest for those who believe." He said, "The thing that has changed my life more than anything else was finally digging my fingernails out of everything in my life that I was trying to control, and letting go of it, and resting in who I am in Christ. And just let Christ work through me and take care of everything. I used to worry about my kids, and how they were going to turn out. I used to worry about money. And when I finally just turned those over to the Lord and dug my fingernails out of them and learned to rest in who He says that I am and let Him live His life through me, I'll never be the same."

I still have men today that were in the room that night tell that story. They'll say something to me like, "Man, when your dad shared that testimony that night, it was a light bulb moment. Things went off in my head." My dad had learned that truth of Sabbath rest, which was a topic Bob covered in his study on the book of Hebrews. This helped my dad understand his identity in Christ. To see and hear that statement from my own dad, a man that I honestly didn't want to grow up to be like when I was a kid, was a significant marker in my progression.

Bob started talking to me about things such as the concept of living by the life of Another. He really started to make the profound simple and the simple profound. I just started seeing life in a whole new way.

At that time, we were attending Living Hope Baptist Church in Bowling Green. The teacher of the Sunday school class we were attending was moving to another state and was going to have to stop teaching. So, one day, one of the associate pastors named Scott Kilgore found me in the hall and said, "I think you ought to take over this class."

My first thought was, "No. I'm a guy that's done this, this, this, this, and this. I don't know a lot about the Bible, so I'm sure not going to stand up in front of a bunch of people and teach." However, after talking to Bob and my dad, they encouraged me to do it. I was scared to death, but I decided that if I was going to do it, then I was going to give it everything I had.

I started diving into the Word. I started pouring myself into the studies that Bob had written. I started hanging out with him even more when I could, and he started to help me understand the most important truth I've ever understood in my life—my identity in Christ. He helped me understand from a scriptural basis that what I do is not who I am, but who I am has a huge impact on what I do.

Now I truly know who I am, and it has forever changed me. It changed every aspect of my life. It allowed me freedom to fail as a husband, father, and an employee of the company I was working for. For the first time, I started getting excited about studying the Word and teaching on Sunday mornings. I started teaching this class. It began with about twenty-five people, and then it started to grow. It eventually grew to over one hundred people, and they had to move it into a different part of the church to accommodate all of them. I had people coming to me saying, "Man, I'm learning things I've never learned before. I'm hearing truths and seeing things in the Word I've never seen before."

And suddenly, I became somebody that people would reach out to for wisdom. Holy cow! Of all people, me! And I kept saying to myself, *"What's happening? What's going on here? This is crazy!"* I was being used as God's mouthpiece, on a weekly basis.

You must understand that nothing is impossible with God. I saw that. I lived it. I went from being a guy who only knew how to quote John 3:16 (and I had to cheat sometimes to even get that right) to becoming this vessel teaching truth to other people, and it was changing their lives. It wasn't me, of course. It was God doing it through me.

I was learning how we really don't have to work our way into a right standing with God. We can rest in Jesus because He died on the cross for us. This allows His Spirit to live in us and lets Him work through us, as we learn to live by His life. This is the Sabbath rest that we have as Jesus followers.

I finally started having peace in my life. I understood that I had gotten peace WITH God when I became a follower of Jesus, but I finally started to understand what the peace OF God looked like. That peace was because of a man named Bob and a man named Jesus. Those two things together took me on a journey that I could have never imagined going on. Bob was just a man—an ordinary, simple man. But if you were around him, you could sense something was different. He lived his life based on the belief that God and a man were capable of anything, if that man were to learn to live by the life of God. Bob constantly would encourage me, "Tim, remember the goal here is to live by the life of Another. You can't love your wife as Christ loved the church, you can't be the kind of father you want to be. But if you learn to live by the life of Another, let Him do it through you, it can happen."

The more I learned to live my life by the Lord's life, the more I became like these men that understood these truths. The more I became like Bob. The more I even became like Jesus. This is a decision a man must make. It doesn't just fall out of the sky. Bob used to always say, "The problem is we don't give God time enough that He might teach us enough so that we might trust Him enough to live by His life that is in us."

You have to say, "You know what? I'm going to spend some time with Jesus. I'm going to spend time with other men, even if that means I don't have time to go to a ball game, or play a round of golf, or whatever." It's a decision.

What happened to me was that my goal became not to know the Bible, but to know the God of the Bible, and the HEART of the God of the Bible. That's important for men to understand. You can know the Bible, and you can quote all the verses you want. However, if you don't know the heart of the God of the Bible, then it's all just information. When knowing God's heart becomes your goal and passion, it changes everything.

I'll be forever grateful for this man named Bob. He taught me, and lived out in front of me, as close to the life of Jesus that I think I could ever witness. He lived by faith. He's written teachings that have gone all over the world. He's invested in literally tens of thousands of people. And he was just an ordinary man that God did something extraordinary through. He was just an ordinary man who decided to pursue God's heart.

Robert "Bob" Glenn Warren passed away on August 25, 2014. Even though he was 68 years old, he would run two or three miles a day, do push-ups and sit-ups, and take really good care of himself. He believed his body was the Lord's temple.

I remember getting the call from a friend of mine in Murray that Bod had suddenly passed away. When I heard this, I just lost it. I got down on the floor and couldn't move. I was stunned. I couldn't understand why the Lord would call this man home without any warning whatsoever. This man who was making such a significant difference in the lives of so many people. I struggled with it.

I went to his funeral at the First Baptist Church in Murray that Friday afternoon. It was one of the largest funerals I've ever been to. They had it live-streamed, because so many people from all over the world wanted to be there but couldn't. All for a simple man in a town of just a few hundred people.

When Bob had started his ministry on The Hill in the late seventies, he took seven young men that were students at Murray State, and they started having a Bible study. One of those seven guys was a young man a few years older than me named Brian Crall. One day I was in Stanford, Kentucky and ran into Brian. We started talking about Bob's passing. I got pretty emotional, and I said, "Brian, I don't get it. I don't know why the Lord called him home right now."

He said, "I know, me too, but I had a dream recently that the Lord gave me that finally helped me put my head around it."

I said, "Would you care to share that with me?" So, he did.

He said, "You know Bob had been a professional basketball player. And those of us that had spent a lot of time with him and discipled under him knew that Bob always had the ball when the going got tough. The other night I had this dream of all these other men in this basketball arena, and there's no other players on the floor, and there's this ball bouncing down the court." He said, "The Lord finally showed me that Bob's mission all along was to prepare men to pick up the ball. And the only way we other men were going to pick up the ball was to know that Bob didn't have the ball anymore. That the Lord had called him home. And that we, as the men that he had invested in, had to pick up the ball and become Bob to other men. Finally, a peace came over me as to why the Lord had called Bob home. It was, 'As long as I leave Bob there, you guys aren't going to pick up the ball. But if I call him home, you guys are going to do what he wanted you to do all along, which was to pick up the ball and go.'"

Those last few times I talked to Bob before he died, he seemed to always get around in the conversation to this same subject. There are so many men out here that know these truths, but they're not telling other people. They're keeping it to themselves. They know, but they're distracted. He said we've just got to get past that and encourage men to get out there and tell other men.

Another takeaway I had from Brian's dream was that when Bob had the ball, he was just one. But if everybody in that arena would pick up the ball, then we could get somewhere, because you've got a whole bunch of people with the ball. The Lord used Bob's death to really increase my sensitivity to this.

I'll be forever grateful for a man named Bob. He was just an ordinary man that God used in an extraordinary way to make a difference. I'm proof of that, and the ripple effect of that.

chapter seven

HERE WE GO

The things which you have heard from me in the presence of many witnesses, entrust these to faithful men who will be able to teach others also.[16]

Afer Bob came into my life, I started being used as a vessel to express and communicate God's truth. About this same time, I read a book by Eric Ludy called *The Brave-Hearted Gospel.* I don't even remember how I got the book. I think I just saw it in a bookstore, and it looked manly, so I bought it. Eric Ludy said something that really hit me at the very beginning of the book:

One of my least favorite words in the English language is castrate. It is a rather awkward word denoting a rather awkward thing...

Castrate: to surgically remove a man's input, potency; his force; his influence; and his strength...

As far as words go, I will readily agree that the word castrate is both ugly and unpoetic...Simply put, there are just no more refined and flowery words that can substitute for it. Emasculate is by far the closest word to fit the bill...However, emasculate has a softer, more disarming feel and therefore can't possibly fully replace the much-needed shock and alarm that oozes out of the word chosen to begin this book.

And as hard as I've tried to think of a better way to lay the groundwork for what this book is all about, I keep coming back to this crazy, ugly word. It says it clearly and concisely, though it may say it with a little too much flamboyance. You see, I believe that the "manly stuff" has been unconsciously removed from the body of Christ today. We are missing the manly input, potency, force, influence, and strength in Christ's body. Some may feel uncomfortable that Jesus was a man, but there is no way around the fact that He was. And yet His body, the church, is strangely lacking the evidence of this fact in our modern Christian world. Jesus has suddenly gone metrosexual in America. He's male, but He's a male that seems ashamed of His masculinity.[17]

The reason you castrate a bull is to take its effectiveness away. Since my dad was a veterinarian, I can relate to that. I can remember, as a kid, going with him on large animal calls and doing the castration of a lot of animals. Again, the purpose behind that was so the male could not reproduce. It also essentially took away the authority from the male animal, because a non-castrated bull was a difference-maker around other cows. It was the authority figure.

We are living in a society today where the Enemy has effectively castrated men. We've become feminized. We've lost our effectiveness, our boldness, and our authority. You see it out there in the movies and on TV. The male figures are depicted as having lost their effectiveness, their authority, their ability to really stand out and be what they were made to be.

About the same time, I read that book, I also read a book called *Finishing Strong* by Steve Farrar. He talks about men being great starters, but how few men finish well in their lives. It's a great book. What got my attention was how many men I knew, and was meeting, that were like that. They started well, but they just didn't know how to finish the race. I saw all these men giving up on their marriages and making stupid decisions, and so much of it had to do with their belief that what they did and what they had was who they were.

One Saturday morning, I was in my office, working on my Sunday school lesson that I was going to be teaching the following day. A client of mine, who was in his mid-'60s at the time, tapped on my office window, and asked me to let him in. He asked what I was doing, so I told him I was working on my Sunday school lesson. He wanted to know what I was teaching that next day, so I shared with him some of the identity truths I had discovered, because that's what I was teaching at that time. It was actually Bob Warren's Romans 1-8 study.

I started to share some of these things with him, and within a few minutes, he got very emotional. He started to tell me that he and his wife had not had much of a relationship for the past fifteen years. In fact, they slept in separate bedrooms. His kids didn't really have much to do with him. They just looked at him as a guy that gave them what they wanted or needed.

He was an extraordinarily successful man. In our community, he was a man that sat on prominent boards, drove the right kind of cars, and looked the part. Most young men would want to be him. That morning, however, he basically told me that he was unfulfilled. He was not sure what was next in his life. He didn't have any close friends. He got emotional, and he started to cry. I got out of my chair, went over, and tried to comfort him while he cried. Eventually, we let go of each other, and he looked at me and said, "I just want you to know, I'm so jealous of you. You've got everything I don't, and I'm heartbroken." We talked some more, and I prayed with him.

It was some 2 1/2 hours later by the time he left. I laid on the floor in my office, exhausted. I was laying there on my back looking up, and I remember praying to God, saying, "Okay God, I don't know what's going on here. I'm not sure what just happened, but please help me not to be that man when I'm sixty-something years old."

I walked away from that thinking, "Here's a man who's got everything the world says you want to have, but he tells me he's jealous of me, a forty-year-old guy who's done everything you're not supposed to do. God is wanting to use me somehow to make a difference." That morning, I promised God that I would do everything in my power to help other men not become that man. And that was the beginning of the mission the Lord was sending me on.

Within a few weeks, in January 2007, Bob's dad, Glenn Warren, passed away. He had just turned eighty-five a few of days before his death. Mr. Warren taught vocational agriculture at three area high schools before he retired in 1976. As far as I know, he never made much more than $30-$35,000 a year. My dad said that next to his own dad, Mr. Warren was the most significant man in his life when he was growing up.

I had met Mr. Warren many times. He had fought in World War II and received a Purple Heart. He was on Omaha Beach at

D-Day. He was with the troops that marched into the Hürtgen Forest after D-Day. I remember him describing the death that he saw in the Hürtgen Forest. It was the longest single battle the US Army has ever fought, lasting about ninety days at the end of 1944. In an area of just fifty-four square miles, the US lost over 33,000 troops. Mr. Warren lost an eye in that battle, but he survived, came back, and started teaching school.

I remember going to his funeral in Benton, Kentucky. I got there late and sat in the back of the Collier Funeral Chapel, which had probably twenty rows of seats. The front two rows were packed with sixty-something-year-old men. They were the honorary pallbearers, and my dad was one of them. As I sat through that funeral, I watched those men and the emotions that they were displaying. It's one of the few times I've ever seen my dad cry. The funeral home was packed, and all to honor a man that never made more than $30-$35,000 in his life. Why? Because he had been such a huge difference-maker. Those men in the front rows had been young men that spent meaningful time with him when they were growing up.

Bob did the eulogy. I'll never forget him talking about his dad. He said, "You know, there were two things about my dad that were so unique. First off, he was the most innocent man I ever knew." He explained what that meant. Bob said, "He was an innocent man that believed the truths of Jesus were the truths of Jesus. He never thought any different. He just believed them and trusted them. So, he had this innocence about him."

The other thing Bob said that was significant about his dad was that he was never in a hurry. He always gave people the time they needed. Those front rows full of those sixty-something-year-old men displayed that. He spent hours and hours with these men in their youth. He invested in them.

I listened to that and watched this play out in front of me, thinking, "You know what? Someday when I'm gone, that's what I want. That's what I want right there. I want that place to be filled with men that I gave my life away to. And that's the reason they come. Not because I was a great businessman, I made X amount of money, or whatever. They come because of what I gave them."

These two events, the older man breaking down in my office and Mr. Warren's funeral, caused me to say, "God, I'm yours. Whatever you want to do, let's do it." That's when we started REUP,[18] a movement for men.

Then God went about showing me some important realities. One of those things was that we had an epidemic of indifference going on. Men were showing an absence of feeling, interest, and concern, because they didn't know their identity in Christ. Men didn't have accountability in their lives. And men didn't have other men in their lives that they'd built relationships with that would cheer them on, do life with them, and be true friends.

This prompted me to step out in obedience and just be used as a vessel. We started REUP and began creating environments and contexts for men to step into. We began helping other men realize that we had a problem. Many problems, actually. For example:

- *Every second of every day, $3,000 is being spent on pornography.*
- *1/3 of men ages 20-30 still live with their parents, a 100% increase in the last 20 years.*
- *The average age of a video game user is 35.*
- *62% of kids are being raised without their biological father.*
- *Only 5% of Christian men ages 39+ say they have a best friend.*
- *Only 3% of a church's congregation are young men ages 18-34.*
- *63% of teen suicides come from fatherless homes.*
- *18-35-year-olds spend more time playing video games a day than 12-17-year-old boys.[19]*

We found that the two main excuses men give for not stepping up to be difference makers are that they don't have time, or they don't know how. Because of this, REUP created tools, resources, and structures to help with those two issues. We started finding ways of dealing with the lie men believe that they can't make a difference because of what they've done or where they've been in their lives. Suddenly, we started to see men react. We started to see men step into what we call "Fire Teams," which is a military term for a small group of men fighting a battle together in a foxhole. They started using these resources to grow in their walk with the Lord. Most men would tell us that they wanted to spend time in the

Word, but they didn't know how. Something was missing. They needed a structure.

The two main words we kept hearing from men were "intentionality" and "structure." If we could figure out a way to give men intentional structure, they would react to it. And they started to do that. Now, years later, there have been thousands of men in numerous states step into these structures and use these resources, and we've seen God do some amazing things.

About this same time my wife and I felt like the Lord was telling us that we needed to make some changes and sacrifices in our personal lives. The first one was to get out of debt. So, we put our house on the market. It was a beautiful old home we'd redone, and a great place to raise our boys, but we both felt like we needed to get out of there and not have any financial burdens on us. It was on the market for over a year, which got us thinking, "Okay, maybe this wasn't what we were supposed to do." Then, two weeks before it was supposed to be taken off the market, we sold it. We had to move out within thirty days, which we did. We were empty nesters by this time, so we moved into an apartment.

REUP was starting to grow as a men's movement. I was traveling to a lot of different churches and companies, speaking to their men. I was still teaching class at my local church. I was also still working with my clothing business. In my mind, I thought things were starting to roll pretty well. I was being obedient to what God wanted me to do, and we had gotten ourselves out of debt.

That was in October of 2010. Little did we know what was about to happen.

chapter eight

WHAT AN OPPORTUNITY!

In January 2011, some ninety days after we sold our house, it felt like the Lord was telling me that to be used more effectively, I needed to step away from the Tom James Company, and a six-figure income, after eighteen years. On Tuesday, the 18th, I called my boss and told him I was leaving the company and that I wanted to make it effective that Friday, the 21st. I told him I would be faxing him over my resignation letter. It was a difficult decision. The company had been so good to me and helped me in so many ways, but I felt confident that the only way I could really do what the Lord was calling me to do was to leave.

So, on Thursday, I had traveled to Cincinnati to make the last deliveries that I would make for this company and I was on my way back to Bowling Green. On Interstate 71, somewhere between Cincinnati and Louisville, as I was passing a truck, I hit a patch of ice. My car spun around, bounced off a guardrail, went off the road, and then rolled down a thirty-foot ravine.

After blacking out for a few minutes, I came to in the car. I was somewhat dazed but could hear noise above me. Apparently, a trucker had seen what had happened and called 911. Within a few minutes, EMT's were rappelling down on ropes to get to me. They got the door off the car and got me out. When they got me up to the ambulance, the EMT informed me that they didn't want to open the car door, because they just knew that I wasn't going to be alive. The car was crunched like a can on both sides. I SHOULDN'T have been alive.

They transported me to the emergency room that evening. Unbelievably, I had no visible injuries anywhere on my body, and no broken bones, but they did a bunch of scans to check for internal injuries. They called my wife for me, and she and my youngest son started to make their way an hour and a half to where I was.

Before they got to the hospital though, the ER doctor came in to see me. He was reviewing my scans with me, and he pointed to a black blob on the screen, saying, "Well I guess you know about this, and then here's what's happened with your internal injuries."

I interrupted and said, "I don't know what you're talking about when you say, 'I know about THIS.'"

He pointed and said, "You don't know about that?"

"No."

He said, "Oh. Well, that is a mass of some kind, about the size of a grapefruit, located in your pelvic area. We just figured you knew about it."

"No, first time I've heard of it."

He said, "Well, maybe we ought to wait until your wife gets here to talk about it a little bit more."

That was the first of many ways that it was obvious that God was going before me. Without the wreck, I would not have discovered the mass until it was too late.

After my wife arrived at the ER, the doctors came in and said, "We can't tell you right off the bat without pathology work and all that, but that mass does not look good." I stayed overnight in the hospital and pondered what was ahead of me. They transported me back to Bowling Green the following day, and I got in to see some doctors. They all told me the same thing. This was not good, and if it proved to be what they were thinking, then my prognosis was bleak.

The day after they found the mass, I called Bob Warren and told him everything that happened. I was on the phone with him for over an hour, crying and pouring it all out. Bob just patiently listened to me. When I had finished, Bob said something I'll never forget. "Tim, I'm so sorry this has happened. It breaks my heart. But I want you to know—what an opportunity all of this is."

I remember responding, "Bob, did you not hear anything I just told you?"

"Yeah I did," he said. "What an opportunity."

I said, "Bob, you're going to have to explain to me what that means, man."

He said, "What an opportunity for Jesus to blow people's minds. No matter what happens." This was not what I wanted to hear from him. I wanted him to feel sorry for me. But he was so confident, so bold. And he said it with such authority.

"What an opportunity."

We exult in hope of the glory of God. And not only this, but we also exult in our tribulations, knowing that tribulation brings about perseverance; and perseverance, proven character; and proven character, hope; and hope does not disappoint, because the love of God has been poured out within our hearts through the Holy Spirit who was given to us.[20]

Within three days I was in Louisville at Norton's Hospital. The head of the pathology department met with me and said, "We need to take a biopsy." So, they tried to do a needle biopsy, and found out that the mass had a strange hard covering and they could not get any tissue from that. They wound up having to open me up, go in and take some tissue from the mass. I was in the hospital nine days as the doctors tried to figure out what was going on. One morning the pathology doctor, who had been there thirty-seven years, came in and said, "I've been doing this a long time. I have no clue what this is." Finally, they decided to send me home as they started sending my pathology to other labs across the country.

Even though I had not had any symptoms beforehand, at this point I started to get really sick. I kept going to doctors, and they kept checking everything, and they kept saying, "Yeah, you're sick. We don't know what's going on. We don't know how to treat it."

Finally, about six weeks later, we found out from the MD Anderson Cancer Center in Houston that it was a rare autoimmune disorder called Castleman Disease. It only affects one in 220,000 people in the U.S. I was diagnosed with the unicentric version of it, which means that the overgrowth of cells was in a single lymph node. Unicentric Castleman disease can usually be treated with surgery, but if the mass is not removed promptly, it can morph into the multicentric version of it, affecting multiple lymph nodes, which is fatal.

We started to meet with specialists and surgeons. I found out that my right iliac artery was wrapped around the mass. As such, there was about an eighty percent chance that I would bleed out and die on the operating table. Four different surgeons who we met with refused to do the surgery. They did not want the liability and the risk.

Meanwhile, I kept getting sicker. I was down from 200 pounds to about 160 pounds. It became my daily accomplishment to get from the bed to the couch. Obviously, I wasn't working. The Enemy started playing with my mind. I have such an appreciation now for those that have mental struggles, because I started having some crazy thoughts, and I went to some very, very, dark places in my mind. Why would God have me go through all of this if I were doing His work? Why couldn't He take away all the pain I was in? Should I just take matters into my own hands and end my pain and suffering in my own way?

The Enemy started using my constant pain as a catalyst to get me to doubt God and get me to have dangerous and harmful thoughts. One particular evening, I was so distraught and deceived by the enemy that I decided I was going to jump out the second story window of our apartment and end all my pain. My wife actually laid over me the entire night and prayed for God to defeat the evil that was lurking all around me.

Finally, in February 2012, we found a team of doctors at Vanderbilt University Hospital who said they felt like they could deal with it. So, we went through that process. The plan was for a team of surgeons to remove a portion of the mass. Then, after the recovery from the surgery, they would attempt to hit the rest with gamma radiation and break it into small pieces. It would be a very risky seven-hour surgery.

The morning of the surgery, the waiting room was filled with family and friends. All of them gathered with me and prayed over me. Then, right before they wheeled me into the operating room, I asked the main surgeon if he would be willing to pray with Mylinda and I. He politely agreed and we all held hands as I asked God to do what only He could do and that His will would be done in that operating room.

A few hours into the surgery, something happened that the surgeons did not expect. The mass detached itself from my iliac artery and just dropped. They were able to remove 98% of it! My wife was there in the recovery room as I awoke. The doctor shared the details about the surgery and said something that he claimed he had never said before: "The only way I can explain this is what the people out in the waiting room were doing—fervently praying! Plus, that unbelievable prayer that you had me pray with you and your wife right before we went into the surgery. There is no medical explanation for what happened."

During the sixteen months of this extraordinary journey with God, I watched as he stripped my self-sufficiency away from me. I literally could not do anything for myself. There were days I was so weak that I couldn't dress myself. He stripped me of every fleshly capability until the only thing standing was Him. I am convinced that He wanted to prove to me that I was His, and that everything in my life had to come from Him.

One of my many times in the hospital in Louisville, I was reading a devotional from *My Utmost for His Highest* by Oswald Chambers. It focused on Revelation 2:4, and the Lord used it to show me what I had allowed to happen in my life.

But I have this against you, that you have left your first love.[21]

He was saying to me, "Tim, I wanted to get you still and get your full attention so that I could remind you that you have left your first love. This is going to be a great opportunity, Tim, not for you, but for me. If you will make me first in your life, I will show you that I AM who I say I AM."

Also, it became clear that the Lord was trying to show my wife and me that true provision is His domain, not ours. He wanted us to understand what I call "the thrill of obedience." He was calling me to be faithful, and to do things that wouldn't make sense to a lot of other people from a worldly view. The only way you can experience the thrill of obedience is to be obedient. The thrill of seeing God do something because you trusted Him is indescribable. Have we done it consistently every time? No. But most of the major decisions we've made over the last decade have been based on obedience and just trying to be faithful.

I would not have experienced this "opportunity," as Bob called it, if I hadn't been in a situation where Jesus could do what only He can do. I would not have understood that principle. He wouldn't have stripped me of my self-sufficiency. He wouldn't have taken my physical abilities away from me at that time. He wouldn't have prompted me to walk away from a significant income and position. If He wouldn't have done those things, I would never have understood that true provision is His domain, or that He rewards obedience. Now I look at most things in my life the way Bob challenged me to look at them, as an opportunity for Jesus instead of something I must somehow fix.

I get asked all the time what I learned during those sixteen months. My answer is always, "God is who He says He is and don't let anything get in front of your relationship with Jesus." You almost have to be a little selfish about that. Because when the enemy finds that he can't defeat us, then he's going to try to distract us from keeping Jesus the main thing. Like my friend Jess Correll says, "If we will jealously maintain our relationship with Christ, it will instruct all the rest of our lives."[22]

It's like in Revelation 2:4, when Jesus tells the church at Ephesus, "But I have this against you: you have let go of the love you had at first."[23] If I have learned one thing, it's that God is who He says He is, and that He is to be our first love. What He wants from us more than anything else is for us to believe and understand this. If we will, then we can look at things from the perspective of "what an opportunity."

I wouldn't wish what I went through on my worst enemy, because I went to some dark places. Yet, I would never have truly learned that He is who He says He is, if I wouldn't have walked through that season, so I'm thankful for that. I wouldn't understand the thrill of obedience without having watched Him do some cool things in the midst of obedience.

As I shared in the last chapter, Bob used always say, "The problem with most of us is that we don't give God time enough to teach us enough, so that we might learn enough to trust Him enough as He lives His life through us." I think that's true. Most of us are out here spending our time trying to be successful at things that don't really matter, so we don't give God time enough to teach us enough, so that we might learn enough to trust Him enough to let Him live His life through us. Sometimes He must get our attention. He did that with me, and I'm so thankful for that opportunity, which I didn't realize was an opportunity until Bob told me to look at it from that perspective.

chapter nine

THE FOGGY BRIDGE

One morning, not long after my surgery in my daily quiet time, I was studying God's call on Moses through the burning bush. Think about Moses. He was a man who made a mistake by killing an Egyptian, ran from that mistake, and wound up being in Midian for forty years. He was out in the wilderness alone with the sheep. Spending all that time under the stars, I feel like he really got to know the God of Israel in a unique, intentional way.

This is kind of what happened to me during my sixteen months where the Lord got my attention, got me flat on my back, and reminded me about my first love. What was interesting to me, though, is that Moses was out there with no distractions. He didn't have the internet. He didn't have Netflix. He didn't have a cell phone, a job, kids running around to different ball games and such to distract him. Yet, the Lord still had to do something that was unusual to get his attention. He had to burn a bush, without it being consumed, and speak through it. I really feel that I was having a similar experience. I was being distracted, and God had to get my attention in His own way.

The other thing that's interesting about the burning bush episode is that Moses was reluctant. He said in Exodus 3:11, "Who am I to go to Pharaoh and to bring the Israelites out of Egypt?"[24] Then in Exodus 4:10, Moses complains of having a "heavy mouth and thick tongue." It's believed Moses had a stutter, or some other speech impediment. Moses doubted himself and his abilities. God's response was to send him anyway. All Moses had to do was just trust God, when He said I AM who I say I AM. Trust that God and a man can make a difference. God didn't give Moses a lot of detail of what was going to happen next, because if He did, it would've scared Moses to death, and he probably wouldn't have done it.

Sometimes He wants us to just act on a word like "Go" or "Come" and trust Him with the details. One day in February of 2013, I was in my quiet time with the Lord. I was on my knees praying and listening, and I had this vision of Mylinda and I walking along with a large group of people following behind us. Ahead of us was a male figure leading an animal. As I observed this figure in front of us, I noticed it was walking along and then would stop and engage people by hugging, embracing, and shaking their hands. Then this figure looked back over his shoulder and made eye contact with me and said two words, "Come on!"

It suddenly hit me that this figure was what I envisioned Jesus would look like. WOW! He was telling Mylinda and I to "come on." Then the vision went away. I was blown away and confused at the same time. It was so real. It was like I could have reached out and touched Him!

What did all this mean? I finally came to the realization and truth that the Lord was calling me to lead something. We just decided to trust Him and "come on," like He had told us to. However, it would be almost another year before He gave us any more details.

My wife described it as though we were on one end of this bridge out in the country somewhere, and we couldn't see what was on the other side, because it was shrouded in fog. We know we're supposed to go to the other side, but we don't know what it's going to look like over there.

I don't think God gives us a lot of details when He wants us to be obedient. If He did, we probably wouldn't do it. We really felt like we were on this foggy bridge. I felt confident that the Lord was instructing me to step away from this company that I'd been with for almost twenty years. We had REUP started by then, and neat things were happening, but it wasn't a way to make a living.

God had proven to me, though, that He was the great provider. Over the years, I had built these relationships with men through the clothing business. Bob had told me a few years before he passed, "Tim, you realize that these relationships you've built are much bigger than selling clothes. There's something more significant there. You have a unique opportunity to encourage and help men to pursue God's heart."

It was through these relationships that the Lord was showing me, "Hey Tim, there's a problem. Men need help. Men need to be encouraged. They need the opportunities to be built. We're not investing in the next generation." I knew I wasn't supposed to just walk away from those relationships. I really felt Him calling me to stay in the clothing business and start my own company.

The night before I resigned from Tom James again (since the first resignation never went through), I wrote in my journal while I was praying, "Okay God, if I do this, you're going to have to take care of me. And everything about this is going to have to be for Your purpose. For your glory." When we were looking for something to call the clothing company I was starting, I went back to this journal entry. We decided to call the company FHG Clothiers, which is "For His Glory," because that's why I did it. I could've stayed where I was and sold clothes, but this venture was going to be used for His glory.

On March 25, 2012, we stepped out and started FHG Clothiers. My friends and family thought we had lost our minds! I had a two-year non-compete clause with Tom James, but the way it was written, it only said that I could not sell clothes within a fifty-mile radius of the town that I lived in. It just so happened that at that time, seventy-five percent of my clientele was outside of that 50-mile radius. So, I was able to honor my non-compete, but still go into the clothing business. I decided not to let people inside that fifty-mile radius know that I was in the clothing business. When they found out, many of them reached out to me, which was not a violation of the non-compete.

So, I was able to start my company and get it going. Throughout that, the Lord really did some cool things. He provided. He looked after me. There was a possibility in leaving Tom James Company that they would come after you and do things to try to cripple you from succeeding. They had a history of doing that to other salespeople who left and started their own company, but it never happened to me. I feel confident that the Lord honored my request about looking out for me, because this venture was going to be used for His glory.

REUP was rapidly growing. Fruit was being produced. Still, I kept feeling like there was something else we were supposed to do.

We were experiencing what one might call a "holy discontent." So, we decided to leave the church of about 3,000 people where we had been for some fifteen years and started looking for something different and seeking more in our journey with Jesus.

We wound up at a little church out in the country that had about fourteen people. I found myself driving a van, picking up kids in troubled areas of town for church. The van had a crack in the windshield, and on rainy days, the water would run through it. I remember saying, "Okay, Lord, what's going on here? I've gone from being very comfortable to this. This isn't me." But He was doing a work. He was trying to show me something.

Not long after that, I felt Him calling me into the role of a pastor. I had fought it and fought it. My wife did not want it to happen. But one night, as I laid in the floor of our extra bedroom crying before God, I finally gave into it. I shared with my wife that I had to do this. God had been so faithful to us. I had to do whatever he was calling me to do. She turned away from her objections and desires and gave her full support. What a blessing she has been! I can't imagine men that feel like God is calling them to His purposes who have spouses that do not support them.

I found a local church, and a dear friend of mine, who was a pastor, who was willing to take me through the ordaining process. At my ordination service, they presented me with a Bible. On the front, it said, "Pastor Tim Brown," which are words I never thought I would see together, especially since I'm a guy that was the most unlikely candidate to have those words engraved on a Bible. But again, it just shows what God and a man can do, if that man desires to pursue God's heart, even at the age of forty-eight!

We still weren't sure, however, what was supposed to happen with any of this. Some friends of ours were feeling a tugging that maybe the Lord wanted something more out of their walk with Him. So, twelve of us started meeting and praying through where God was leading us. We felt like He was leading us to start a church.

So, in September 2014, we fulfilled what the "Come on" vision had been about by starting a church in Bowling Green. The last thing our town needed was another church. What it did need was a different church—a church whose mission was to change the way people view the church so they can develop a growing relationship with Jesus. I became the lead pastor. Since starting the church back in 2014, we have been on a journey not really knowing what it's supposed to look like. The bridge is still foggy, but we're just trying to be faithful and obedient.

What's interesting is not long after we started the church, I got asked to do some fill-in preaching at two different churches back in my hometown of Murray. As I stood upon the stages of both those churches, I could see people out in the crowd that knew me from my younger days. I remember a couple different instances where people would come up to me after the service and say, "You know, our pastor announced that some guy named Tim Brown was going to be preaching this Sunday, and the only reason I came today was to see if it was the Tim Brown I knew, because I just knew there wasn't any way it could be THAT Tim Brown."

I just laughed and told people, "Yeah, you're right. I never dreamed I'd be here too." I still looked the same on the outside, but what it validated to me was what God could do to a man's heart, and that He could literally take any man and use Him, if that man will learn to live by His life. I got the thrill and the opportunity to preach in front of many people that used to know the "old Tim Brown." But now they were getting to see the new creation that scripture talks about:

> So then, if anyone is in Christ, he is a new creation. The old has passed away. The new has come![25]

I have since developed relationships with a lot of these men that knew the "old Tim Brown," and they have now been affected by the "new Tim Brown," via my being the conduit of the Lord. Some of these were men I used to party with and do things that we'd be really embarrassed by if people knew about them today. But now I get to experience this love for Jesus with them as well, which is cool to see. The other thing my wife and I have seen walking this foggy bridge is that obedience is just the willingness to try something uncomfortable. It was uncomfortable for Jesus to crawl onto that cross. It was uncomfortable for Him to be beaten like He was beaten, to have the skin ripped off of Him. My uncomfortable, compared to that, is not significant.

The other thing I want a man to understand is that embracing "uncomfortable" is one of the ways to experience Jesus in the way He wants you to experience Him. Men need to get over the fear of being uncomfortable to really be difference-makers. It was uncomfortable for me to leave that church and step into driving that van for a church with fourteen people that was in a converted horse barn, but it was one of the greatest ways for me to learn some things about Jesus that I needed to learn.

Fear is one of the most motivating factors in a man's life, whether it's the fear OF something, the fear of DOING something or the fear of NOT doing something. Fear must be embraced. Fear is walking into the fog on the other side of the bridge. For a man to truly be a difference-maker, he's going to have to step into some fog every now and then. He's going to have to step into uncomfortable.

Men don't like change. I believe men are more emotional than women; we just don't let it show. Men must constantly ask God to give them a foggy bridge in their lives. God doesn't often give us many details. And that fogginess, that fear that the enemy creates—we can't be afraid to step into it. I honestly think the reason most men won't step onto the foggy bridge is because they believe that what they do is who they are. Because of that untruth they won't take a risk and step into their destiny that is hidden on the foggy side of the bridge.

However, as we learn our identity in Christ and live by His life, we can embrace what the Apostle Paul wrote to the church at Corinth. I love the way God inspired Paul to write. Paul was a man's man and yet he was not afraid to express his emotions and passions:

> *Either way, Christ's love controls us. Since we believe that Christ died for all, we also believe that we have all died to our old life. He died for everyone so that those who receive his new life will no longer live for themselves. Instead, they will live for Christ, who died and was raised for them.*
>
> *So, we have stopped evaluating others from a human point of view. At one time we thought of Christ merely from a human point of view. How differently we know him now! This means that anyone who belongs to Christ has become a new person. The old life is gone; a new life has begun!*

And all of this is a gift from God, who brought us back to himself through Christ. And God has given us this task of reconciling people to him. For God was in Christ, reconciling the world to himself, no longer counting people's sins against them. And he gave us this wonderful message of reconciliation. So, we are Christ's ambassadors; God is making his appeal through us. We speak for Christ when we plead, "Come back to God!²⁶"

These verses nail it! We must learn to look at other men from Christ's perspective, not with an earthly view. Jesus only puts people in one of two buckets—saved or lost. We must look at people from this eternal perspective. If I look at a man from Christ's view, uncomfortable doesn't matter. We have been given this message of reconciliation. We are Christ's ambassadors!

I've found that men are challenged when I ask them this. "Why would you want to wake up every day and be like everybody else? As a man, why would you want to do that?" That doesn't sound manly. That doesn't sound like an adventure.

What sounds like an adventure is, "I'm going to be different today. I'm going to step into that fog. I don't care how uncomfortable it makes me." That sounds like an adventure. Men like adventures. Men like to be challenged. So, our goal should not be to wake up in the morning and try to be like everybody else.

I honestly believe that men have settled for so little in their lives. I say this often, "Men are great settlers." We settle for so little. John 10:10 says He came that we might have life and have it abundantly. We must quit settling for things if we ever want to experience that abundant life. The way we have that abundant life is to intentionally step into uncomfortable.

I am reminded of that story a Holocaust survivor tells of when the Jews were packed on a train like cattle, being transported to the concentration camps. He remembers the train stopped in the middle of a town, and there was a church they could see through the slits in the railroad car. The people were in the church having a service and they were singing. The lights were on so the people in the railroad car started screaming out for help. And he said the louder they screamed, the louder the people in the church sang to drown out the noise, because they didn't want to come out and help them. They were scared. They would have had to do something they weren't comfortable doing. So, the easy route was to drown out the noise of the cries for help.

We're living in a world today where young men are crying out for help. And when we won't step into the fog, we're just turning up the noise and drowning out the cries. We are too comfortable, and it shows. Therefore, crossing the foggy bridge is critical for men to become who they want to be. I can validate that, not because I'm anybody important, but because I've stepped into it myself. Bob used to always tell me, "The greatest adventure of your life will be pursuing Jesus." And I can say that's true.

PART FOUR
THE WAY FORWARD

chapter ten

A BROKEN HEART

For the eyes of the Lord move to and fro throughout the earth
that He may strongly support those whose heart is completely His.[27]

G od is searching for those whose hearts are completely His.
Think on that for a minute. While you are sitting there
reading this book, His eyes are looking for a heart that is completely His to strongly support. He is not imposing any require-
ments on you to clean up your act, or anything like that.

God is looking. He wants to use you and me to help write His
story. He deeply cares about your family, your friends, and your
co-workers, and He wants you to care deeply as well. He wants you
to want to be a part of writing His story.

If your heart is truly broken for what breaks His, then He will
do amazing things through ordinary people like you and me for
His extraordinary glory.

I want you to join me on an adventure of becoming people
that God is looking for, people whose hearts are completely His.
I believe we are at a pivotal time in history and our world needs
broken-hearted Jesus followers more than ever.

I've already told you about one serious medical issue that I was
faced with. However, on October 18, 2018, I literally found out
what it means to have a broken heart.

That day, I had been working in my hometown of Murray. My
oldest son and his family live there, and I had stopped by their
home to visit. I had just sat down on the couch to read a book to
my five-year-old granddaughter, when I started experiencing pain
in my chest, neck, and shoulder. As the pain increased, I broke out
in a heavy sweat and became short of breath. My daughter-in-law
immediately called 911. Unbeknownst to me, I was having a major
heart attack.

An ambulance took me to the hospital in Murray, then I was rushed forty-five miles to a larger hospital in Paducah. It just so happened that the cardiologist was there and had just finished a procedure. They alerted him that I was en route via ambulance, and he was waiting for me when they wheeled me into the ER. He immediately took me to the catheterization lab, and they discovered I had a one hundred percent blockage in my left anterior descending artery, which is known as the Widow maker. I also had a ninety-nine percent blockage on the right side. They did a procedure to stent all the blockages, two in the Widow maker and one on the right.

Afterward, the doctor who did the procedure told me that I should have come through the hospital doors with a sheet over me. He had never seen anybody live longer than thirty minutes after a heart attack of this magnitude, and it had been over an hour before they got me to his hospital. He said it was a miracle that I was alive. Someone was really looking out for me and apparently wasn't done with me.

A few days later I started on a journey of asking God why He was so gracious to me and was keeping me around. I remembered something that Bob Warren had said—"In God's classroom, you will repeat the class until you pass it."

This was not a class that I wanted to repeat, so I figured some review was in order. I started by going back through my daily prayer notebook. Here are some of my entries from a few days before the heart attack:

- *Sept. 30th—help me to hear your voice—**break my heart**— give me more boldness, more humility, more compassion— remove my pride—give me joy again—Am I really trusting you? The way you want me to?*
- *Oct. 2nd—**break my heart**—work out my time/schedule/the details—make prayer the most important thing I/ We do—give me/us clarity—Increase my passion for you—help me not to forget my first love (YOU).*
- *Oct 3rd—provide for us in your way—build your church and deepen our desire for You—**Break my heart for what breaks yours**—help me to hear Your voice—sort out my roles and responsibilities.*

• *Oct. 8th—What do you want above all else?—**break my** **heart**—help me to love everybody always—give me more boldness, authority, compassion, humility—Increase my desire for You and to know Your heart—give me joy.*

Do you see the pattern?

For some reason, the day before my heart attack I had written out 1 Corinthians 2:2. *"For I have decided to know nothing among you except Jesus Christ and Him crucified."* Also, I had written on that day to make sure to review my desire statement daily.

The desire statement was something I had come up with a few years earlier. The concept is based on Psalm 37:4, "Delight yourself in The Lord, and He will give you the desires of your heart."[28] My desire statement signifies what I want most, what I have a deep longing and craving for. This is in the front of my planner, and I read it every day:

I desire to know Him! Not just head knowledge. But to know His desires—His heart—His longings—His wisdom. I desire to spend whatever time HE allows me on this earth to be a "Bob" in some way to others. I desire to have the kind of peace, discernment, compassion, and intensity that Bob had. I desire to not be in a hurry and to have time for others. I desire to empty my bucket into other men's buckets. I desire to focus on helping Travis and Tyler to be men that desire to know God's heart. I desire Mylinda and I to grow deeper in love with HIM and each other. I desire for my grandkids to know that that Poppa loved Jesus and their Mammy. I desire to not worry about provision and the "stuff" in life.

So, I started asking the Lord, "Why are you so gracious to me? Why are you keeping me around? Obviously, it's not so I can sell more clothes. Why then? Why me? I'm just a knucklehead that has done everything you should not do, that ran from you for years and thought that I was Superman and could do what I wanted, when I wanted, to whom I wanted."

Eventually, I arrived at a different question. "What do you want me to see, hear, and do?"

I felt the Lord impress this upon me. "Tim, look at what I have done in your life. If anyone can validate that I AM who I say that I AM, it's you, Tim. You're still around because of that! I'm gracious to you because I want you to be gracious to everybody you ever come eyeball to eyeball with and show them what Jesus really looks like. I'm gracious to you so you can boldly say that you have lived out the equation that JESUS plus nothing equals everything! I'm gracious to you so you can have the authority to tell others that MY grace is sufficient and is the greatest gift known to man! I'm gracious to you because I want to live MY life through you so I can unleash the simplicity of Jesus in everything you ever say or do! I'm gracious to you so you can seek ME and MY heart each day I continue to let you have breath! I'm gracious to you so you can rock your granddaughter to sleep and kiss her soft cheek. I'm gracious to you so you can take your grandson to Tractor Supply and buy him a trailer for his toy tractor. I'm gracious to you so you can have the desires of your heart, which are my desires, as you learn to live by my life that's in you and let me do my work through you and totally trust me with every area of your life! I'm gracious to you so you will love others as I have loved you and constantly ask yourself what love requires of you, because love has no loopholes or agendas. I'm gracious to you so your heart will break for what breaks my heart!"

I thought, "Okay, Lord, I get it! Now what am I supposed to do with that? What do you want? What is the message here? What is the way forward? Apparently, I'm not the sharpest knife in the drawer, Lord. What is the answer? What is this message you want me to share with as many people as I can?"

I found out the Lord sometimes has a sense of humor when He answers. You really shouldn't ask Him for something if you don't want it to happen. I didn't hear Him speak audibly, but I felt him press upon me, "Tim, I gave you the answer. The answer is a broken heart! And I broke your heart physically to make my point. Wherever your heart is focused is the direction I will move or let you move. But if your heart is not focused on My heart, I will let you move that way too, because you're not a robot. I gave you a free will. You will make your own choices."

When a heart is truly broken it should create a strong drawing or pulling action. It's almost like you can't control it. It just pulls you in. A broken heart should keep me from being too wrapped up in the details of my life to focus on God's heart and God's will. A broken heart should keep me asking if I am really caring about the people around me at the level God cares. A broken heart should keep my focus on the only two things that last forever—God's Word (The Truth) and human souls (People).

Our hearts will be broken for what breaks God's heart only to the degree we intentionally spend time with Jesus and others. We just need to figure out a way to spend most of our time on the only two things that are eternal—truth and people. I'm convinced that we are a by-product of our time spent with Jesus (the truth) and our time spent with people. We are also a by-product of the time we DON'T spend with Jesus and people.

Because of the time I have spent with Jesus and with people, I have made a decision that will drive me the rest of my life. The faith of the next generation is worth anything and everything. The faith of the next generation is worth asking God to break my heart for what breaks His. The next generations are crying out for those whose hearts are completely broken to give them something to hold onto. Therefore, I believe the way forward is a broken heart. Why is this important? We, the Church, are at a crossroads. For some reason, we keep doing what we have been doing over and over and expecting different results. We are not relevant in our culture anymore. In fact, sometimes, we're the laughingstock of our culture. Why aren't we asking God to help us change the world?

We all have a calling on our lives. A broken heart is essential to embracing that call. We are BORN to serve our Creator and others. Try not to cheat yourself out of this most wonderful calling!

I want to go back to one of my life verses, which I used again at the beginning of this chapter:

> *For the eyes of the Lord move to and fro throughout the earth that He may strongly support those whose heart is completely His.*

This verse makes it clear that His eyes are looking for a man whose heart is completely His, but in response where should our eyes be?

...fixing our eyes on Jesus, the author and perfecter of faith, who for the joy set before Him endured the cross, despising the shame, and has sat down at the right hand of the throne of God. (Hebrews 12:2)

Fixing = aphorao (turn the eyes away from other things)

His eyes are looking and we have a response, we either look away or we FIX our eyes on Him!

I also think it's important to give you some background on this verse. The context of it goes back to chapters 14-15 of 2 Chronicles, and it centers around a king named Asa. Asa was a good king at a bad time. There was idol worship in Judah, and people were sacrificing children to these idols. Horrific things were going on, and most of the kings were involved in it. There was a long cycle of kings, and few of them were good kings.

We see in chapter 14 that Asa develops a heart for God. He removes the idols. He starts cleaning things up, and God sees Asa's heart. Why? Because God is searching. Then we see that God brings a test Asa's way. The Ethiopian army of over a million men come against Asa, and Asa thinks, correctly, that this is an impossible battle to win. So, he prays this prayer in 2 Chronicles 14:11:

"Lord, there is no one like you to help the powerless against the mighty. Help us, Lord our God, for we rely on you, and in your name we have come against this vast army. Lord, you are our God; do not let mere mortals prevail against you."[29]

God answers Asa's prayer, and they accomplish this amazing victory. Then in chapter 15, God sends a prophet named Azariah to tell Asa that the Lord was pleased with him and "if you seek Him, He will be found by you, but if you forsake Him, He will forsake you."[30]

We see that Asa and the people encountered about twenty more years of peace and economic success, and he removed most of the idols that people were worshipping. Asa had gotten comfortable by then. He had lost his desire for God's heart, and he was kind of doing his own thing.

Then in the thirty-sixth year of Asa's reign, Baasha, the king of Israel, came against Judah. Asa decided he could take care of this himself without depending on the Lord. So, he entered into a treaty with Ben-Hadad, the king of Aram, to take care of King Baasha and his men. Israel withdrew from the land, and all was well. Then we pick up with verse 7 of chapter 16:

> *At that time Hanani the seer came to Asa king of Judah and said to him, "Because you have relied on the king of Aram and have not relied on the Lord your God, therefore the army of the king of Aram has escaped out of your hand. Were not the Ethiopians and the Lubim an immense army with very many chariots and horsemen? Yet because you relied on the Lord, He delivered them into your hand.*[31]

Then, Hanani the seer shared with Asa this principle of God that weaves throughout the Bible as well as our world today.

> *For the eyes of the Lord move to and fro throughout the earth that He may strongly support those whose heart is completely His.*[32]

"Asa, make your heart His," is what Hanani seems to be saying. "Not just once, but constantly. Don't rely on the world. Don't set your desires on the world's desires. Don't make it all about you and your desires because God is searching."

Unfortunately, Asa didn't respond favorably to Hanani's message. We see that his life ended in a sad way, with a severe disease in his feet that lasted two years, and a great window of opportunity closed. You know, this is a common story, in that most people start well but finish poorly. Why is that? I'm convinced it's because we quit seeking what breaks God's heart. When we do that, our hearts harden instead of softening. Our hearts' desires become our own desires instead of God's desires. What are God's desires? Have we pursued His heart enough to even know what He truly desires? I think we can figure it out based on what Jesus said:

> *Father, I desire that they also, whom You have given Me, be with Me where I am, so that they may see My glory which You*

have given Me, for You loved Me before the foundation of the world.[33]

What is Jesus' desire? "I desire that they be with me where I am." There is only one way that happens. It is through Jesus Christ. If this is what Jesus desires, then it's what the Father desires, because Jesus is one with the Father. Is that our desire? Should it be?

We must be continually focused on asking God to break our hearts for what breaks His. Did you notice what I had put in my prayer journal entries consistently? "Break my heart." I know if I don't ask Him that, my heart will harden instead of softening.

You know what else happens if we don't continually ask God to break our hearts for what breaks His? We become indifferent and quit taking risks. We quit stepping into uncomfortable. All we want to be is comfortable. We lose the air in our sails. We miss out on so many blessings. The next generations behind us start losing their way because our hearts aren't broken for them.

If we don't keep a continual focus on what breaks God's heart, we wind up becoming a good moral person on cruise control. We become a Sunday Jesus follower and we miss out on SO much of what God has for each one of us. I don't want to wind up in that place. I want to make a difference until the day I die, because Jesus has changed my life. I know God and a man can make a difference. And I know you want to make a difference as well, because we were made in His image.

The question is...Will we answer this call? Will we embrace the opportunity at this pivotal time in history? We are seeing things going on we never imagined possible. God's not surprised. He's not up there wringing His hands, but it blows our minds, doesn't it? God IS working. He is searching, and He is waiting for us to join Him.

But are we so wrapped up in the details of life that we haven't really focused our hearts on God's will? Do you and I want personal happiness and prosperity ahead of what God wants?

Let me ask that question again because it probably left a mark. Do you and I want personal happiness and prosperity ahead of what God wants? I know the answer to that question, and I'll bet you do, too, if you're honest. That's why we're not effective in this culture, because we look like everybody else—out there busting our chops to get all that stuff that doesn't matter.

This leads to an important question. What needs to change? Well, if God never changes, then I guess that leaves...ME! But what does this look like? Where do we start?

Here's a better question. Why does asking Jesus to break our heart scare us so much, when it's the one thing He wants more than anything from us?

This is how I define a Jesus-broken heart. It is a God-given concern for others that propels us out of our comfort zones. It is a passionate concern for God's agenda that supersedes our own desires for personal peace and prosperity.

Ask most people what they want, and they might say they all want peace, a nice house, a nice car, nice stuff, and they become passionate about it. However, if we're Jesus followers, the most passionate thing in our lives should be God's agenda—not our own personal happiness, our own prosperity, or our own personal peace, but God's agenda.

I believe we need to call a time out in our lives. We need to take an honest look at what our lives consist of, the busyness that is keeping us from what God wants for us. I call this doing a practical fly-over of our lives. We like to complain about how busy we are, but we need to ask ourselves what is keeping us busy? Kids' activities? Hobbies? Work? Something else?

How do we solve the busyness problem? (Fair warning—this is the part where I go from preaching to meddling.) Would fewer things help? Let me ask a question to the parents reading this. Who signed the kids up for all the things that keep you so busy? Who said your kids have to do all those things? Is there a rule out there somewhere that I didn't know about? Or for you workaholics out there—why are you working so many hours? Is it so you can keep up with the Joneses? Who said you have to live in that house? Who said you had to drive that car?

Most of us, men especially, are out here trying to be successful at things that don't really matter and won't ever really matter. We all have choices, and many of us are living a life that is making us miserable because of our own choices. That's not what God wanted for us.

Something else we need to understand is that we need to change **our** world before we can change **the** world. I believe one of the reasons why the church isn't being relevant is because we, as individual Jesus followers, aren't willing to change **our** world.

We must quit saying things like, "I will do it later." "I will make those changes when the kids get a little older." "I want to ask God to break my heart, but if He were to lay something on my heart, I wouldn't have time to do it." " I will do it when I have more financial resources."

You mean the financial resources that you're using to spend on your own personal pleasures most of the time? You know what you'll do when you have more of those financial resources? You'll do more of the same. Some Jesus followers are the greediest people I've met in my life. They think it's all theirs, and it's not. This is why Psalm 24 begins:

The earth belongs to the Lord. And so does everything in it.[34]

It's His, and He's letting you have it for a little while. Just admit the problem is that you have busied your life to a point where you can't spend time with Jesus or intentional time investing in others. Identify the things you can start to eliminate. Then, quit talking about it and do it!

Most of our lives are full of stacks, full email inboxes, and to do lists. We think the answer is working harder and longer. However, that never seems to work. It takes a paradigm shift. We must be intentional. We have to draw some boundaries then focus on the things that bring about growth in our life, our marriage, and our kids. It won't happen overnight.

I've determined that most people are flashlights. They're like diffused light going in multiple directions with high frustration and lack of productivity. We need to be laser beams. Those that have a laser focus learn how and why to say no to certain things and focus on the right things. Do you realize a laser beam can cut through a steel door when it's that focused? A flashlight can only show light a little way across a room.

What could happen if we stopped all the busyness and embraced Paul's words in Colossians 3:1-4?

Since, then, you have been raised with Christ, set your hearts on things above, where Christ is, seated at the right hand of God. Set your minds on things above, not on earthly things. For you died, and your life is now hidden with Christ in God. When Christ, who is your life, appears, then you also will appear with him in glory.[35]

Set your minds and hearts on things above. He says it twice to make His point!

Jesus also tells us how to be intentional:

Do not store up for yourselves treasures on earth, where moths and vermin destroy, and where thieves break in and steal. But store up for yourselves treasures in heaven, where moths and vermin do not destroy, and where thieves do not break in and steal. For where your treasure is, there your heart will be also.[36]

Here is a truth that most of you are not going to like. *Our behavior tells what matters.* Louie Giglio puts it this way:

So how do you know where and what you worship? It's easy. You simply follow the trail of your time, your affection, your energy, your money, and your loyalty. At the end of that trail you'll find a throne; and whatever, or whomever, is on that throne is what's of highest value to you. On that throne is what you worship.[37]

Our behavior tells what matters. It hurts, but it's true. This doesn't have to be a negative statement, though. We can always change our behavior which, in turn, changes our direction. It's vital to understand that direction will determine destination.

Have this attitude in yourselves which was also in Christ Jesus, who, although He existed in the form of God, did not regard equality with God a thing to be grasped, but emptied Himself, taking the form of a bond-servant, and being made in the likeness of men. Being found in appearance as a man, He humbled Himself by becoming obedient to the point of death, even death on a cross.[38]

Jesus was living in the ultimate comfort of heaven, receiving the adoration of angels. He saw our need, left His comfort zone, and stepped into mankind. He crossed a barrier into uncomfortable just to let people know that God loves them.

Paul also wrote about his own attitude toward the lost:

> *I am telling the truth in Christ, I am not lying, my conscience testifies with me in the Holy Spirit, that I have great sorrow and unceasing grief in my heart. For I could wish that I myself were accursed, separated from Christ for the sake of my brethren, my kinsmen according to the flesh.*[39]

Wow! He is saying that he would be willing to lose his salvation and be separated from God, if all his friends and family could be saved. What about you?

I know it's hard for us to care for others at that level, but do we have a glimmer of concern for them? Do we care enough to rearrange some things in our lives? Do we care enough to step into things that make us uncomfortable? Do we care enough to use our financial resources for others instead of using them on our own self-indulgence and pleasures? If we don't care enough to the point of changing some things in our lives, then God can't strongly support us. And this is what He wants to do.

We need to care not only with our thoughts, but also with our behaviors and actions. I'm not trying to make anyone feel bad about themselves, but I want to challenge you to spend some time doing a personal fly over. Then ask God to help you because that's what He wants for you more than anything. He wants you to have the blessings that He's got in mind for you. He wants us to live the abundant life.

> *The thief comes only to steal and kill and destroy. I came that they may have life and have it abundantly.*[40]

Now, He probably won't break into your world and say, "Okay, you have to sell everything you have, move to the other side of the world and go live in a hut." He won't overwhelm you. But start asking Him to break your heart for what breaks His, and He'll do it. He will ask you to make some changes; I'll guarantee that. But they will be changes that will matter and be fulfilling. And you will experience Him like never before.

THINGS WE SHOULD KNOW MOVING FORWARD

1. Try to spend at least 30 minutes each day in God's Word and in prayer. If your lifestyle is such that this cannot be accomplished, you are too busy and need to make changes in your daily routine (Psalm 1). Suggestions: Try to sleep less; think of ways you can meditate on God's Word even while accomplishing other tasks.

2. Learn to view material possessions in relation to the time it takes to purchase them, as well as the time it takes to maintain them (Psalm 90:12; Ephesians 5:16). If you will divide the price of an item by what you make per hour, you can determine how many hours of your life it will take to possess the item. Remember: **Time is precious!**

3. Avoid going into debt for items that depreciate in value. Be very wise when considering borrowing capital for items that appreciate in value. In fact, live a debt free life if at all possible—and yes; it is possible (Proverbs 22:7).

4. When deciding on a job, consider more than the salary. Also consider how much overtime will be required of you (Ecclesiastes 2:4-11). No retired person that I have known has been sorry they didn't work more hours. Most are sorry they didn't spend more time with their families and with the things of eternal significance. Also, it is a job that you can leave at the office, or one you will have to take home with you?

5. If you have children remember that a child spells the word love — "**T-I-M-E**." Also make sure to spend time with them doing the "unspiritual" things—like going to their ballgames or doing things with them that interest them outside of "Christian activity" (Colossians 3:21).

6. Have someone hold you accountable all your days. There is much safety in accountability. It was when David was no longer accountable that he fell into sin (2 Samuel 11:1).

7. Take time at least four days a week to exercise (walk, run, play tennis, swim, etc.) Bodily exercise is profitable (1 Timothy 4:8), for the mind thinks more clearly when the body is in good physical condition.

8. Try to encourage at least one person each day. By encouraging others, we become encouraged.

9. Spend more time being a friend to God that being a friend to others. It is when you become intimate with your Creator that your horizontal relationships will take on new meaning. In other words, the path that leads to intimacy with others begins in the heart of God (Philippians 3:10).

10. Ask the Lord to give you neither poverty nor riches (a moderate lifestyle in other words—Proverbs 30:7-9). If you can learn to live moderately you will avoid the pitfall of always wanting more (Proverbs 27:20). You are wealthy if you can learn to be content with less.

11. When making decisions, get counsel from more than one person (Proverbs 11:14; 13:10; 15:31). There is much safety here. You will find that those who love you enough to sometimes disagree with you are friends indeed.

12. You will never give to God more than He gives back to you. Make it a habit to give to those in need (2 Corinthians 9:6, Proverbs 11:24; 19:17; 22:9).

13. **Always** remain teachable. I am convinced that one of the major roadblocks to spiritual maturity is an unteachable spirit.

14. Make it a habit to read through the book of Proverbs at least once every six months. There is a wealth of practical truth in this book. Also try to read (or pray) at least one Psalm each day.

15. _View yourself as God views you_. You are a saint who sometimes sins, and not a dirty sinner saved by grace. At the point that you gave your life to Christ, God made you into a person who is as righteous (right) in His eyes as He Himself is righteous (2 Corinthians 5:21). In fact, He made you into a finished product—He glorified you (Romans 8:30).

Note: This was taken (with permission) from "**40 Things We Should Know and Teach**" by Bob Warren (the man who discipled me).

chapter eleven

REPENTANCE

Most of us have been unconsciously squeezed into the mold of our culture and have begun to think like a consumer instead of a committed Jesus follower who's all about God's agenda. Most of us, though not on purpose, have neglected the clear teachings of God, which say:

A nd do not be conformed to this world, but be transformed by the renewing of your mind, so that you may prove what the will of God is, that which is good and acceptable and perfect.[41]

This is so counterintuitive to our human nature because we live in a culture where we're taught that it's all about us. We're number one! However, it is vital that we embrace this truth Paul talks about and become who God made us and called us to be. You see, we all have a calling on our lives. The Lord has impressed upon me that a broken heart is essential to embracing that call. We are born to serve our Creator and others. We are not born to try to accumulate as much stuff as we can. Try not to cheat yourself of this most wonderful calling!

In the last chapter, we talked about doing a practical flyover of our lives. Once we do this, we can name the things that are keeping us from focusing on God's agenda. Then we are ready for the next step.

We must genuinely repent. Genuine repentance brings about a shattering realization and leads to a broken spirit. Genuine repentance is that change in our mind which leads us to turn from our ways and desires to focus on His ways and desires. It is a repentance so deep and radical that it affects the whole spiritual nature and involves the entire personality. The intellect must function, the emotions must be aroused, and the will must act.

This is the first step of learning to live by His life in us. Here's what that looks like to me. I will get on my knees and say, "God, I'm sorry I'm making it difficult to let you live your life through me. Restore my way, Father. Purify and cleanse my heart of the world. I recognize I have become too much like the world. I don't look at people the way Jesus looked at people, which was either Lost or Found. My heart doesn't break for them. I'm sorry, Father. Help me!"

This isn't about shame or beating yourself up. When you genuinely repent, it allows you to go to Him with confidence. This is what He wants for you. Genuine repentance gives us a restored view of God Almighty.

When we dare to set aside our pride and agendas, to stop pretending, to recognize we have lost our way, and to ask Him to help us be who we are called to be, then He takes care of the rest. He'll set us free. Our view of God is refreshed. He does all the hard stuff and heavy lifting, and we are free to love and pursue His desires instead of our own.

Where can we go to get an example of this kind of broken spirit? An example of a heart that breaks for God's agenda? I think an ordinary man from the Old Testament gives us that example. Nehemiah was that ordinary man. He was not a prophet or a priest. He was a business guy. He held the role of cup bearer to King Artaxerxes, and he had become one of the King's closest confidants.

This was during the time of the exile of God's people. They had been dispersed throughout the nations because they had given into the pressure of idol worship, among other things. But God had promised that someday He would regather His people. The book of Nehemiah begins like this:

The words of Nehemiah the son of Hacaliah. Now it happened in the month Chislev, in the twentieth year, while I was in Susa the capitol, that Hanani, one of my brothers, and some men from Judah came; and I asked them concerning the Jews who had escaped and had survived the captivity, and about Jerusalem. They said to me, "The remnant there in the province who survived the captivity are in great distress and reproach, and the wall of Jerusalem is broken down and its gates are burned with fire."[42]

We see that he immediately asked questions about the people and the city. He was immediately concerned for God's people and His city. People that are focused on God's agenda ask questions and gather information.

If you could go back in time and see the condition of the city of Jerusalem, you might conclude that God's agenda was dead. His promises weren't really going to come to fruition. It reminds us of our world today—the violence, the division, the hatred, the lack of empathy, the indifference towards the hurting, the desire to pursue things that don't matter. It's what Jesus warned us about in Matthew 24:12:

There will be such an increase of sin and lawlessness that those whose hearts once burned with passion for God and others will grow cold.[43]

Then and now, I think you might ask the question, "Where is God in all of this?" The answer has always been the same. He is on His throne as well as living inside each Jesus follower. Better questions might be: "If God didn't move, then why have we stopped responding to Him? Have we become indifferent? Is our love growing cold?"

Nehemiah could have said, "I hate everything that's going on with God's people, city, and agenda, but I have this important job that is taking most of my time. Plus, I need to be able to satisfy MY desires and wants. I didn't create that mess. I don't even live in that city. And who am I? I'm just an average Joe. I can't make a difference. I'm just one person. I mean, I do have the King's ear. I do have some influence, but I've learned to keep my mouth shut. I don't want to jeopardize my job. Surely somebody else will help."

He could have thought that way, but he didn't. Look at his response:

When I heard these words, I sat down and wept and mourned for days; and I was fasting and praying before the God of heaven.[44]

When we look at our world and see the condition of it and how God's agenda is going down the tubes, is this how we respond? As we try to take practical steps to be one of those people that God is searching for, we need to stop and really look at Nehemiah's response and see what we can learn from it.

He stopped what he was doing and sat down.

It wasn't like when we're flipping through the channels, and we see a World Vision or Compassion International commercial and turn the channel. Or when we hear about a young man or woman struggling with an addiction and we hope somebody's not going to ask us to get involved. Or when we see a young lady who is pregnant and the daddy has hit the road and turned his back on her, we react by saying, "Well, you know. She made her own bed; she'll have to sleep in it. Should've made better decisions. Boy, I sure hope they don't ask me to get involved with that."

Nehemiah stopped what he was doing and sat down. He let his attention and focus be on the problem. He got still so he wouldn't be distracted. He let his heart connect to the problem. Then....

He wept.

You weep when your heart is hurting. Nehemiah's life was working out great. He lived in the palace, the gated community, the subdivision that you needed to live in to be somebody. He was comfortable. But he got the news that God's agenda was failing, and his heart responded. He wept. He was genuinely concerned. It hurt him to hear this news. Then...

He mourned.

Mourning has to do with grief. It's the feeling that things shouldn't be this way. We could replace the word "mourned" with "grieved". God's people, God's city, and God's agenda were slowly slipping downhill. People were hurting, lost, and searching for answers. They were looking for hope. He mourned and grieved because of that.

Then he acted. But look at the very first action he took.

He fasted and prayed before the God of heaven.

He knew he needed to hear God's voice to direct him. He realized the only way to do this was to fast, that is, to stop eating for a time and give God his full attention. He realized he needed to be able to distinguish God's voice over all the other voices around him.

We see that Nehemiah was moved. His heart was broken. Because of that, God propelled Nehemiah out of his comfort zone. Look at the emotion in Nehemiah's reaction to the news he heard.

> *When I heard these words, I sat down and wept and mourned for days; and I was fasting and praying before the God of heaven. I said, "I beseech You, O Lord God of heaven, the great and awesome God, who preserves the covenant and lovingkindness for those who love Him and keep His commandments, let Your ear now be attentive and Your eyes open to hear the prayer of Your servant which I am praying before You now, day and night, on behalf of the sons of Israel Your servants, confessing the sins of the sons of Israel which we have sinned against You; I and my father's house have sinned.*
>
> *We have acted very corruptly against You and have not kept the commandments, nor the statutes, nor the ordinances which You commanded Your servant Moses. Remember the word which You commanded Your servant Moses, saying, 'If you are unfaithful I will scatter you among the peoples; but if you return to Me and keep My commandments and do them, though those of you who have been scattered were in the most remote part of the heavens, I will gather them from there and will bring them to the place where I have chosen to cause My name to dwell.'*
>
> *They are Your servants and Your people whom You redeemed by Your great power and by Your strong hand. O Lord, I beseech You, may Your ear be attentive to the prayer of Your servant and the prayer of Your servants who delight to revere Your name, and make Your servant successful today and grant him compassion before this man."*[45]

He cried out to The Lord with a heartfelt plea for God's loving-kindness and for God to hear his voice. When was the last time you pleaded for God to hear your voice on behalf of somebody else? He interceded for them by confessing their sins. That's what you do when your heart's broken. Nehemiah also acknowledged God's promises, asking Him to remember them. Then, He asked God for success in the critical next step.

We need to recognize that Nehemiah took a risk here. However, God granted Nehemiah's request to the King. If you read chapter 2, the King responded when Nehemiah wanted him to, because he had asked God to make that happen. He was willing to risk his job to ask the King to help God's people, and the King granted his request.

Remember earlier I said we quit taking risks when we stop asking God to make His desires our desires? Nehemiah was a risk taker. What about you? When was the last time you took a risk for the God that sent His son to die for you? On the surface, taking a risk sounds more exciting than not taking a risk. Bob used to say to me, "Tim, why in the world would you want to wake up every day and be like everybody else?"

Most people don't want to take a risk but let me tell you this— a God risk is the right risk. Always! A great movement to fulfill God's will has always started with one person who cared deeply enough to seek and hear God's voice and then stepped out and did something. That person understood they couldn't change everything, but they were convinced they had to change something. So, they got uncomfortable and took a risk.

Nehemiah had a God-given concern that propelled him out of his comfort zone. He had a passionate concern for God's people and God's agenda that superseded his own personal comfort and prosperity. These are the people God is looking for. These are the people God will use to change this culture and this world. You were made to be one of these people, and the enemy is either going to defeat you or distract you. You must recognize this and embrace this calling on your lives.

See this isn't about doing something great for God. It's about letting God do something great in our hearts. God never does something great *through* us until He does something great *in* us! For God to really make a difference through us, we must allow Him to deeply move us, not just in our thoughts, but also in our behaviors and actions. We must come to Him with genuine repentance and a broken spirit.

chapter twelve

STEPPING OUT

Sometimes when I watch the news or read the paper, the things going on in our world look so daunting, so hopeless … the evil that is at work … the abuse of children, women, and others. I get discouraged and think the world has never been this bad. The church has never been so anemic. I start to whine and complain and even feel like giving up at times. How about you?

Then God reminds me of the same thing He told King Solomon:

> *That which has been is that which will be, and that which has been done is that which will be done. So there is nothing new under the sun.*[46]

Throughout all of history, God has raised up ordinary people to do extraordinary things. In Old Testament times, He raised up Moses and Elijah. In the Middle Ages, when the clergy did not understand or declare the gospel, Martin Luther ushered in a reformation that reintroduced discipleship to the Church. Thomas Paine said of the American Revolution, "These are the times that try men's souls." Yet, God raised up countless leaders to fight in the War of Independence, but also to fast and pray for victory for the American colonies.

God is always searching, and God is always working. Not only does He do extraordinary things through ordinary people, but many times, He does it through people that assume God will pick somebody else. But as we have discussed, God only has one qualification to be one of those difference-makers—to be a man or woman whose heart is fully broken for what breaks His. God is searching for people who are willing to take a radical step of faith, people who will choose to step out to fulfill God's clearly defined will at great personal risk and sacrifice.

Nehemiah was one of these people. We see in Nehemiah 2 that he took a radical step of faith and decided to step out to fulfill God's clearly defined will at great personal risk and sacrifice. His step of faith seemed somewhat crazy to most people who were watching, but we will learn that this sort of thing is the next step in being who God created and called us to be.

Let's pick up our storyline with Nehemiah 2:1-5:

> *And it came about in the month Nisan, in the twentieth year of King Artaxerxes, that wine was before him, and I took up the wine and gave it to the king. Now I had not been sad in his presence. So the king said to me, "Why is your face sad though you are not sick? This is nothing but sadness of heart."* **Then I was very much afraid.** *I said to the king, "Let the king live forever. Why should my face not be sad when the city, the place of my fathers' tombs, lies desolate and its gates have been consumed by fire?" Then the king said to me, "What would you request?"* **So, I prayed to the God of heaven.** *I said to the king, "If it please the king, and if your servant has found favor before you,* **send me to Judah,** *to the city of my fathers' tombs,* **that I may rebuild it.**"[47]

Let's go back for a minute. We can all probably relate to being nervous to speak directly to a king, but we need to appreciate that Nehemiah took a huge risk here by not being happy in front of the king. The servant's job was to make the king's life great and to keep him happy! A servant could have lost his life if he weren't accomplishing that on a particular day. And the king noticed that Nehemiah was sad.

Nehemiah admitted he was fearful, but he didn't let fear stop him. He took a radical step of faith by asking for the king to send him to Judah. Remember, Nehemiah was living in the castle, the gated community, the right subdivision, the right side of the tracks, but he requested to leave that ultimate comfort to go to a city that was in ruins. Why? His heart was broken. He had a broken spirit and was focused on God's agenda, not his own. Nehemiah knew what God's will was—for the city to be rebuilt, God's promises to be fulfilled, and God's people to be regathered. It was God's clearly defined will. See, it's okay to be afraid when God is moving you toward something. So, you're in good company if you've ever been through that.

A radical step of faith is choosing to take a step into God's clearly defined will at great personal risk and sacrifice. There are people that do this, but most do it reluctantly. It is counterintuitive to our human nature, to how the world has programmed us, and to how the enemy has distracted us. However, with a broken heart and spirit, it becomes one of the most natural things to do.

We should clarify that a radical step of faith is not some crazy, emotional, knee-jerk reaction. Faith is trusting in God's character whether you feel like it or not. Our faith is what God deeply desires.

> *And without faith it is impossible to please Him, for he who comes to God must believe that He is and that He is a rewarder of those who seek Him.*[48]

Our activity itself is not what pleases Him, but He does want us to act on our faith. Where there is no risk, there is no faith. The goal is not to be good; it's to trust Him. If our hearts are broken for what breaks His, we will take radical steps of faith that will make people think, "What in the world is going on with them?"

Our culture needs some Jesus followers willing to take some crazy steps of faith. We must deny ourselves and trust God instead of always trusting in our own understanding. It might look a little crazy to others, but honestly, with as many times as I've been called crazy in the last fifteen years, I'm okay with it. Jesus' whole family thought He was crazy! This world needs some Jesus followers willing to quit worrying about what other people think about them and concern themselves only what pleases God, which is faith.

Another of my favorite examples of a radical step of faith in scripture is the calling on an ordinary guy named Elisha. Let's pick up his story where he meets the prophet Elijah:

> *So, Elijah went and found Elisha son of Shaphat plowing a field. There were twelve teams of oxen in the field, and Elisha was plowing with the twelfth team. Elijah went over to him and threw his cloak across his shoulders and then walked away. Elisha*

left the oxen standing there, ran after Elijah, and said to him, "First let me go and kiss my father and mother good-bye, and then I will go with you!"

Elijah replied, "Go on back, but think about what I have done to you." So Elisha returned to his oxen and slaughtered them. He used the wood from the plow to build a fire to roast their flesh. He passed around the meat to the townspeople, and they all ate. Then he went with Elijah as his assistant.[49]

Try to visualize what Elisha's life was like day in and day out. Plowing the field up one row, turning around, coming back down the next. The view never changed. Neither did the smell, I expect. Can you relate? Wouldn't it be nice to step out of ordinary? Elisha got that opportunity. Elisha was being faithful with the task at hand. God wants to reward those who are faithful with the little things. So, in the middle of Elisha's ordinary routine, God sent Elijah to take Elisha from where he was, to present him with an opportunity to take a radical step of faith.

> *"Elijah went over to him and threw his cloak across his shoulders and then walked away." (v. 19)*

A cloak was a covering made of animal skin. Symbolically, it said to Elisha, "That which has covered me will now cover you. As God has worked through me, He will now work through you."

If we apply what we read about here in 1 Kings 19, there are two key principles we must embrace as we move forward.

1. You don't have to fully understand God's clearly defined will to fully obey Him immediately.

You don't have to have all the details to be obedient. Look what Elisha did.

> *Elisha **left** the oxen standing there, **ran after** Elijah, (v. 20)*

Notice he didn't have to pray about it. He didn't get out a legal pad and make a list of pros and cons. He didn't consult with his board of directors. We are great at overthinking and talking ourselves out of things that the Lord has laid on our hearts. Elisha just believed that God was in it and said, "That's enough for me!"

2. God will use more of those who are willing to hold on to less.

We must be willing to dig our fingernails out of some things that we are trying to hold onto. Here is how Elisha demonstrated this principle.

> *So Elisha returned to his oxen and slaughtered them. He used the wood from the plow to build a fire to roast their flesh.* (v. 21)

This sounds a little weird and maybe a little icky as well. God was calling Elisha to follow this prophet Elijah, whom God had done great things through. In fact, God was calling Elisha to do greater things than Elijah had even done. But before he could do any of these things, he needed to do something that didn't make a lot of sense. Craig Groeschel, Senior Pastor of Life.Church, says it this way....

Elisha needed to.... **"Kill the cow and burn the plows!"**

In the culture Elisha was living in, sacrificing the cow was a ceremonial sacrifice that represented letting go and trusting God. Cows were a vital entity to function and survive back then, so Elisha was sacrificing something that was probably one of the most substantial things that he had in his life.

What would correspond to that in your own life? Prestige? Living in a certain house or neighborhood? Power or influence? A title? A job that pays well but takes you away from your family most of the time? Remember, God isn't trying to take something from you. He wants something better for you! The thing is, you must be willing to let go of what's good to get what's best, because He will use you more if you hold on to less.

What about burning the plows? What does that represent? I believe Elisha was communicating, "I am burning Plan B and trusting God. There is only one plan, and it's Plan A." The "plows" in our lives are what chain us to the ordinary. But God doesn't want ordinary for us. He wants us to have life and to have it more abundantly!

Society teaches us, "You need to keep your options open. Maybe you ought to hold onto the cows and plows just in case this trusting God thing doesn't work out." That's not faith. Without faith, it is impossible to please God. We need to be people willing to take a radical step of faith. The world doesn't see that in us. They see most of us just going through the motions, showing up on Sunday to get our ticket punched, and going home.

In scripture we see people doing crazy things. We see them willing to let go and not hold onto things that could hinder the way forward. David walked away from his flocks. Peter let go of his fishing business. Matthew, the tax collector, walked away from the great income that he had (from cheating people). All of the Apostles left everything! They killed every cow and burned every single plow in their lives. You think God strongly supported them? Those twelve men changed the world. Those twelve men are a big part of why you're reading this book in the first place.

Now, a word of caution about killing cows and burning plows. We must be sure it is God's voice we are hearing before we strike the match! The way we do that is simple. We make sure that what we feel He is moving us towards lines up with scripture and what He desires. Anything outside of that is potentially problematic. For example, there was this guy that I coached Little League football with when the boys were little. He said he felt like the Lord was calling him to quit his job and coach Little League football. There's crazy faith and then there's just plain crazy.

We must be careful, but even so, God's call on our lives is immediate and thorough. He doesn't want us looking back. Sensing a radical step of faith is never an accident or a mistimed part of our life. When He calls, it is the appropriate time to turn our hearts to Him and respond.

Over six years ago, Mylinda and I sensed God was prompting us to leave our comfortable little Jesus-following world and step into uncomfortable by leaving our church of 3,000 people for a church of fourteen people. To step out in obedience though, we had to decide we were going to kill the cow and burn the plows. A few months later, twelve of us started meeting and praying on Sunday mornings in a bank meeting room and ended up starting the church I pastor now. That was the hardest thing I've ever done in my life, but it was also one of the greatest things I've ever done in my life. I burned the plow. I killed the cow. I'm never going to be the same. I can't go back.

The thrill, the fulfillment, the passion to know His heart has been amazing! But to continue stepping out in faith, to keep embracing the way forward, some of us need to let go of our "blankie." To put it another way....

Sometimes to truly step into your God given destiny, you must let go of your security.

Are you willing to do that? I believe the greatest enemy of the greater life God has for us is...us! To be the people God is looking to strongly support, it's time we start taking risks and making decisions the world doesn't understand. They may think you are a little bit crazy, but Amen! Because too much ordinary isn't getting us anywhere.

If we read the remaining chapters of the book of Nehemiah, we see that because of a man whose heart was broken for God's agenda, God did something extraordinary through Nehemiah and the people in Jerusalem. God strongly supported them, and they rebuilt the wall around Jerusalem in fifty-two days. This was an architectural miracle. It should have taken months, if not years, and they did it in fifty-two days! There was a tremendous revival of God's people. God's agenda was back on track. What looked impossible when they watched Hebrew News Network or read the Jerusalem Times became a reality that was totally different. One man, whose heart was truly broken helped change the lives of hundreds of thousands of people.

So can you! Actually, so can God through you as He strongly supports you, even as you go about making your heart completely His.

chapter thirteen

CONTINUAL OBEDIENCE

I searched for a man among them who would build up the wall and stand in the gap before Me for the land, so that I would not destroy it; but I found no one.[50]

It is evident from this verse that God is searching for someone willing to stand in the gap. He is looking for someone whose heart is completely His.

In the last three chapters we have been unpacking what it looks like to be someone whose heart is broken for what breaks God's heart. In this chapter, I want to look at the last step in becoming one of those people—Continual Obedience.

Let me ask you a question. Do you feel, for the most part, that you have peace in your life? God's kind of peace? Can you sleep well at night because you have peace? Over the last few years, I have had more peace in my life than at any other time. You could take a lot of things from me, but don't take my peace. I'll fight you for that!

Why do I say that this peace is so important? I think John gives my answer at the beginning of his first letter:

What was from the beginning, what we have heard, what we have seen with our eyes, what we have looked at and touched with our hands, concerning the Word of Life—and the life was manifested, and we have seen and testify and proclaim to you the eternal life, which was with the Father and was manifested to us—what we have seen and heard we proclaim to you also, so that you too may have fellowship with us; and indeed our fellowship is with the Father, and with His Son Jesus Christ. These things we write, so that our joy may be made complete.[51]

Until we become continually obedient, and continue moving forward, we're not going to see a lot of the things that God wants us to see and share with others. We'll miss out on so much. John shares that he has experienced Jesus and wants to write this so others might have the same experience, which would complete his joy. I believe this is an expression of fullness and peace in his life.

I want to ask this question to you. Do you want others to experience the great joy and fullness and peace of Jesus? Do you want to experience this for yourself? Why don't we experience it more often? I believe it's due to a lack of continual obedience. Obedience is what allows us to experience Jesus in new and fulfilling ways. We may not get all the details, so we're going to have to take a radical step of faith to be obedient. We're probably going to have to genuinely repent of some things that are distracting us from God's agenda. Most of us are so self-centered that we wake up each day thinking of ourselves and how our wants and desires can be met. Oh, there are times that I feel convicted and think about others for a little while, but then I go right back to thinking about me.

As I look at scripture, I see that this is exactly what Satan wants us to do. He doesn't mind me writing this book, and he doesn't mind you reading it as long as we don't ACT on it. As long as we are not obedient, he doesn't care if you never miss a Sunday at church. As long as you don't act on what you've learned, he doesn't mind Bible studies or small groups if we just go about our business focusing on our own little Christian bubbles. Therefore, James admonishes Jesus followers:

> But prove yourselves doers of the word, and not merely hearers who delude themselves.[52]

Are we ever living in the age of hearers! When it comes to obedience and action though, we start looking for somebody else to do that. See, Satan hates action. He hates change. He hates us being obedient. This is why genuine repentance is so important. It brings about a shattering realization that we are putting our own desires above God's desires.

The core of John the Baptist's message was repentance. Change! Take action! Turn the other way and go! What did Jesus teach?

Repentance. What was the first thing Peter taught on the Day of Pentecost? Repentance.

You're probably familiar with the story in Luke 18 about the rich young ruler who encountered Jesus. He asked Jesus what it takes to get to the kingdom of heaven, and Jesus told him to sell everything he had and follow Him. But instead of following Jesus he went away sad. He was convicted but walked away without being obedient. Jesus said it was hard for a rich man to enter the kingdom of heaven. "Rich" doesn't necessarily mean a certain amount of money, so much as an unwillingness to let go of the money one has. It's hard for those not willing to let go to enter the kingdom of heaven, and the rich young ruler wouldn't do it.

Remember what we learned in the last chapter—God will use more those willing to hold onto less. The rich young ruler wouldn't let go of his wealth, so God couldn't use him. We see another example of this in Luke 19, when Jesus encountered Zacchaeus. Zacchaeus was an extraordinarily rich chief tax collector. Jesus basically had the same conversation with him that He had with the rich young ruler. We see a difference in verse 8, however, because Zacchaeus decides to change, not just hear:

"Zacchaeus stopped and said to the Lord, "Behold, Lord, half of my possessions I will give to the poor, and if I have defrauded anyone of anything, I will give back four times as much."[53]

See the difference in these two examples? Obedience! One was willing to change, not just hear. The difference was realizing it would cost something but obeying anyway. The times in my life when I was courageous enough to change and be obedient to Jesus have been some of the greatest times in my life. Were they easy? No. But they've been some of the greatest times of experiencing Jesus. Here's an important principle.

You can't let the cost of your obedience dictate your actions!

My church wouldn't be here today if the twelve people who decided to start it with me had counted the cost and chosen not to act. REUP men's movement wouldn't be changing men's lives if that was the case. You and I wouldn't spend eternity with Jesus if He had considered the cost before He crawled on that cross willingly.

We must come to a point in our walk with Jesus when we have a Popeye moment. Some of you reading this will remember Popeye; some of you will have to Google it. In all the old Popeye cartoons, Bluto would mess with him. Popeye would let it go for a while, but then he'd finally get to a point where he'd say, "THAT'S ALL I CAN STANDS! I CAN'T STANDS NO MORE!" Then he'd bust open that can of spinach, and it was lights out for Bluto!

God allows us to get to a point in our lives when we have such a lack of peace that we must decide to change, especially when God lays something on our heart, and we keep pushing it away. We've got to decide to embrace those things. They may not make sense. You may not get a lot of details. It may cost you something. We must understand that we can't change everything about that situation but be convinced we have to be obedient to God's desires and God's agenda.

I remember being so convicted after my encounter with that older gentleman in my office that I told you about in chapter 8. I remember being so burdened by his story, to the point where I went to Mylinda and said, "I gotta do something to help other men not become that guy. Would it be okay if we started empowering men somehow?" That's all I can stands, and I can't stands no more! Ten years later, we've had thousands of men affected by this movement.

My heart was burdened by the statistics about record numbers of young people leaving the church and the next generations losing their way. That's all I can stands, and I can't stands no more! I went to Mylinda and said, "Let's start a church that believes the faith of future generations is worth anything and everything."

> *"Slowly but surely I began to realize the truth. I had loved and admired and worshipped Jesus without doing what He had said...I wanted to actually do what Jesus said to do."*
> —Katie Davis Majors

In 2006, 18-year-old Katie Davis went to Jinja, Uganda to serve at an orphanage for the summer before she started her freshman year at Vanderbilt. While she was there, she saw rag-poor parents hand their children over to the orphanage so the kids could get three square meals a day and an education. She witnessed families being ripped apart. Katie didn't wait for someone else to do something. She saw a need and said to God, "Here I am. Use me." Instead of going to Vanderbilt to start her freshman year of college, she did something. Katie ended up pioneering a sponsorship program, including meals and school fees, to keep over 600 kids in families. She started a school feeding program for a few thousand more. She still lives over there. You can check out her ministry at www.amazima.org. *Amazima* means "truth" in Luganda, the local language.

Here is a fact that I see quite often. Our present generation is the most unchurched generation in modern history. How can we just go home and sleep like a baby if that's the case? We must decide enough is enough. That's all I can stands, and I can't stands no more!

We must take a step of obedience. As Katie Davis said, we must want to do what Jesus said to do.

And Jesus came up and spoke to them, saying, "All authority has been given to Me in heaven and on earth. Go therefore and make disciples of all the nations, baptizing them in the name of the Father and the Son and the Holy Spirit, teaching them to observe all that I commanded you; and lo, I am with you always, even to the end of the age."[54]

We were told by Jesus to go and make disciples. It's a big deal when we obey and do it. It's an even bigger deal when we don't.

Why aren't we doing this? We read those verses above, and we're like, "Eh, okay." It makes no sense to me that I believe in hell but am not warning people about it and showing them the way out. Oh, I can justify it. "Well I'm a pastor. I'm supposed to equip the saints, and they can go out and do it." Wait a minute, preacher boy! You believe in hell. You know you're not going to hell, because you're a Jesus follower, but it doesn't bother you enough that other people are going to go there? There's something wrong with that.

What about you? Have you shared the gospel of Jesus with anybody lately? Have you ever? Does the thought of someone going to hell when you could have prevented it not bother you? Why not? "I'm scared Tim. They might not like me anymore. I'm afraid others might think I'm a fanatic or something." Oh, so you're more worried about your comfort than their eternal destiny? "Well, I wouldn't know what to say." Well, what did Jesus say? **"I am with you always."** If you go and be obedient, He'll take care of the rest. Look at Mark 16:20:

> *And they went out and preached everywhere, while the Lord worked with them and confirmed the message by accompanying signs.*[55]

My goal is not for you to put this book down feeling all sad and beat up. My goal is for you to change and experience the thrill of obedience and a peace and joy like no other. Obedience is when you experience His presence. The Holy Spirit was given to be a witness. You want to experience His presence in your life? You want to have the peace I've talked about? You want your joy to be complete?

GO!!!

Will you have to give up something? A hobby for a season? Certain relationships? Getting to watch SportsCenter? Maybe some of your financial resources? Yes, you probably will have to give up some of these things. But the thrill of obedience will replace and be more fulfilling than all that stuff, and you will get to experience His presence in a way you never imagined.

Will it be easy? No, it will likely be the hardest thing you've ever done. Will it hurt a little? Probably. Will you get disappointed? Absolutely. Will somebody break your heart? Count on it. Will you see tons of people's lives changed? Maybe, maybe not. Bringing in the harvest is God's job. We just need to get busy planting the seeds. There will be a lot of uncertainty, but I can tell you one thing. You will have an amazing peace.

But in the midst of that peace we must come to this realization—sin is so ugly! We have no clue how ugly. Most of us just see the outer rim. We don't see the pit. But I'm telling you, that pit is real, and it should scare us. If we just focus on the outer rim, it's easy to think life's a bowl of cherries, and somebody else will take care of the problem...they don't need me. We've got to decide that enough is enough. I can't stands it no more!

Satan would be fine with you reading this chapter, being sad and convicted for a few hours, then going back to your normal. As a matter of fact, I feel like when people hear the truth, it's almost like Satan is in Vegas with his little gambling hat on, and he's pushing all of his money to the middle of the table, betting it all on one thing—that you will read these words and do nothing. You know why he's betting that? Cause that's what we usually do. The odds are in his favor.

Doing nothing is the easy way out.

Silence in the face of evil is evil itself. God will not hold us guiltless. Not to speak is to speak. Not to act is to act.

Not to act is the way backwards. But how about embracing the way forward? What if everyone reading this embraced what I'm writing about here? You think things could be different? Absolutely!

Twelve guys changed the world. One man named David stepped onto a battlefield, killed a giant, and because of that, within minutes, thousands of men were impacted. See, Satan has convinced us that one person cannot make a difference in the world, and that is so far from the truth. God and A Man can make a difference. It only takes one man or woman that is pursuing God's heart. He's looking to strongly support that individual, and He will blow our minds.

We just need to identify the things that are distracting us from God's agenda, genuinely repent of those things, take a radical step of faith and trust God, then go about living a life of continual obedience as He goes with us.

PART FIVE

OUR DAYS ARE NUMBERED

chapter fourteen

FOUR FUNERALS

A man's days are numbered. You know the number of his months. He cannot live longer than the time You have set.[56]

Teach us to understand how many days we have. Then we will have a heart of wisdom to give You.[57]

We all know death will come knocking someday. What we don't know is the time and place or the ways and means. An exercise that I have been a part of in the past was writing my own eulogy. How would I want to be remembered? It's amazing to me that when we think of how we want to be remembered, and then compare it to the reality of our lives as they are, they don't really line up.

Over the past few years, I have officiated three funerals and attended a fourth that have made a lasting impact on me. *(Note: any names mentioned below have been changed for privacy of the individuals and their families)*

Side-Road Sam

Sam was a good friend who was a part of REUP's leadership team. He was also part of my Fire Team, the group of men I met with each week. I had met him when he and his wife visited a Sunday School class I was teaching. Shortly after that, Sam reached out to me to have lunch. We started occasionally having breakfast and lunch together and struck up a friendship. I guess you could say we were kindred spirits.

Sam worked for a corporate company in Nashville and was a very skilled leader and communicator. He had two boys that he invested a lot of time in. He loved his family and was passionate about helping his sons become great men.

One day, Sam shared with me what he called "living a parallel life." He described that his walk with the Lord was like being on a side road that was running parallel to the Interstate of Manhood. It was as if he could see the main road that he wanted and needed to be on but couldn't find the on ramp. He desperately wanted to be on the main road, but just couldn't figure out how to get there.

I gave him the challenge to pursue God's heart. We started meeting together and hanging out. For seven years, I watched his passion for the Lord take him over completely. He shared with me later that once he accepted this challenge, he started to see himself on the main road of being the man he wanted to be. Learning his identity in Christ, and that what he did was not who he was, transformed everything about his life. I got a front row seat to see God take a man who was stuck on the side road and using him to make a difference.

Sam embraced every opportunity to step into uncomfortable for the sake of future generations. He took countless young men under his wing at REUP men's events. He became one of those men that God was searching for.

Then one morning in our Fire Team gathering he informed us that he was having some tests done for some discomfort he was having in his throat. It was soon discovered that he had esophageal cancer. He started treatment and endured that for a while, but he never showed much, if any, progress. Within a few months it had spread to various other parts of his body.

I got the privilege of sitting by his side a few days before the Lord called him home. He told me that he was tired of fighting and wanted to go home to Jesus. I cried and told him I loved him and that I would honor his life by making sure the legacy of his sacrifices to future generations and REUP would live on. He shared with me that what John 8:32 says was so true. The truth had set him free!

I was humbled to be asked to speak at his funeral. Following are excerpts from my notes from that day:

I was a man who loved Sam dearly and who had the honor of having him as a giant of a friend in my life. As I started praying about the best way to honor Sam today and what to say, the Lord in His grace gave me a thought—just share what Sam would say if he were standing here before all of you today. So, for the next few minutes, I want to share with you what I think Sam would say if he were now.

First, Sam would say, "Cancer did not win! I am standing face to face with God almighty and praising Him! I've seen Jesus, my earthly dad...oh what a glorious past few days!"

Secondly, I think Sam would say, "Don't be sad for me. I got to be loved like you cannot imagine by family, friends, co-workers, and church family. They loved me ferociously. I was the most blessed husband and father in the world."

Next, I think Sam would turn his attention to men. He had such a passion and burden for men to be who God created them to be! And he would first say, "Guys, it's okay to turn in your 'man card' and go to a "non manly" concert," because that made his wife happy, and as husbands we should strive to do the best we can to make our wives happy!

Then he would say, "Quit trying to live by your life. Let Christ that is in you live His life through you!" I saw that happen in this man. As much as I am a gas pedal, Sam was a good brake for me. During leadership meetings when I would be charging ahead filling the room with big ideas, Sam would stop me and remind all of us that we couldn't do any of this planning on our own. Only God living through us could make the difference.

He would say, "Ask God to burden your heart for the next generations. They need us!" Sam loved to pour his life into young men. He coached. He led small groups. He was a dedicated worker and leader for the boys' football and baseball teams. He took a large number of young men under his wing that he met through REUP's men's events that we call FACEMASK.

In Paris, Tennessee, earlier this year, a group of high school football players wanted to start a Fire Team. Sam paid for all their materials, called them, and encouraged them. He did that for several groups of young guys. He knew these next generations were our future and he wanted them to know Jesus!

Fathers, be your kid's hero! Sam loved his sons so much. He talked about them all the time. He showed them the way, and he will live on for many years through these young men.

Men, quit making excuses and be men of your word! It really bothered Sam when men failed to show integrity. I can remember numerous calls and texts from him when he would be so mad because a guy hadn't followed through on what he had said he would do. Just think about Sam's life. He had a two-hour commute every day. He spent time daily with his wife, did things with the boys, coached ball, served in church and REUP, and was in a Fire Team every single Friday morning at 6:30 AM. This guy was busy, but he NEVER went back on his word!

Next, he would say, "Go Cats!" because this guy loved the Big Blue, the Kentucky Wildcats. And he would tell you that if you are ever in Gadsden, Alabama, be sure and have a fried bologna, egg, and cheese biscuit from Jack's!

A few weeks ago, in one of the last things Sam wrote for REUP's blog site, he talked about losing his voice. I want to read a portion of that for you now:

"Right now, I don't know when, or if, I will speak normally again. My voice, which is one of those things I took completely for granted 15-16 weeks ago has been taken from me. I use that voice daily in my vocation and I am limited right now in what I can do there. I help to lead a small group of teenage boys at church and I've been unable to do that. I can't even conduct a normal conversation with someone sitting right in front of me. For the

past five or six years of my life, I have tried to take my role as a disciple-maker seriously. I have tried to say yes to opportunities that would put me in the right places to make disciples. Have I done enough? Absolutely not! Can I ever do enough? Absolutely not! Even so, God had given me a voice for a reason. Now I regret not doing more when I had a voice. Not for one moment did I ever imagine that one day that voice might no longer be there. Maybe with more time and treatment my voice will return. Maybe it won't. I guess what's in my thoughts today is to encourage every one of you that has a voice to use that voice for His glory. Use it for the most important reason it's been given to you. Tell people about Jesus. They need to know, and you have the ability to tell them."

Finally, I think Sam would say that if somebody here today isn't sure about this God thing, he would want you to know that God is who He says He is, and the most significant thing you can ever do is give your life to Him. Make Him your life so you are no longer having to live your own life! Accept Jesus as your Savior so you can truly understand Philippians 1:21, "To live is Christ and to die is gain".

For those of us know Jesus as our Savior, I think Sean would challenge us with these words from Luke 10:27-28:

> *The man answered, "'You must love the Lord your God with all your heart, all your soul, all your strength, and all your mind.'*
> *And, 'Love your neighbor as yourself.'"*
> *"Right!" Jesus told him. "Do this and you will live!"*[58]

Sam lived. I got to see it firsthand. God and a man can make a difference!

What are you going to say about my dad tomorrow?
In February of 2017, my father-in-law passed away at the age of eighty-eight. He had never been in the hospital for an illness until the last three days of his life. He was an active man and hardwork-

ing, taking care of a large farm and house by himself until the very end. Bobby had farmed most of his life and also worked in a stove manufacturing plant for many years. He was a hard worker and a no-nonsense guy when it came to work and finances. He married the love of his life and they had sixty-seven years together before she passed away a short time before him, and together they raised a large family with five children and many grandchildren.

He was what many would say was a hard man, but he also had some good under the tough exterior. He seemed to be unhappy most of the time I was around him. I'm not sure if that was true, but that was how I perceived it. He had very few friends. Around the community, he was known for being difficult to be around, because his temper and anger would sometimes get the best of him. Even his relationship with his own kids was difficult at times. He wasn't the type of man that showed his affection, or any affection, with words or touch. When my wife and I started dating, I was honestly scared to death of him. He would hardly speak to me, and when he did it was very short and kind of gruff. I don't think it was until near the end of his life that he really ever began to respect me.

Bobby was very conservative with money. Some might even say "tight." Making money and holding onto as much of it as possible was very important to him. I suppose this made sense based on the way he had grown up during the years of the Great Depression. Like a lot of men, I think he believed that with a certain level of assets you could not only have material things but the respect and standing of your peers. And with only a 10th grade education, he did very well in the eyes of the world.

Now don't get me wrong, he had good qualities as well. There was never a time he turned one of the kids or grandkids away if they needed help. He anonymously helped people at this church. If he saw a need that he could fix either physically or arrange for it to be taken care of, he would. Mylinda and I are grateful when we look back over the years and remember how we were helped in our times of need.

I was asked by the family to officiate a portion of his funeral. I'm still not sure what he would have thought of that! The evening before the funeral as we gathered at the funeral home for the visitation, I was approached by one of my wife's sisters. She said something to me that still resonates today: "I want you to know that I don't envy you. I am praying for you and the task ahead of you. I know it's going to be difficult to talk about my dad tomorrow in an uplifting way."

She didn't know how right she was. A few hours later in bed, Mylinda rolled over and asked me if I was still awake. I said that I was, and I told her what her sister had said. My wife looked at me and said, "I'm just laying here staring up at the ceiling trying to think what you're going to say tomorrow about my dad. I am struggling to come up with a whole lot of things for you to say." WOW! These were his own daughters! And they were right. I was having a hard time coming up with what to say about this man. At the funeral the following day I did the best I could at honoring him. Thank goodness another pastor was involved, so the whole burden didn't fall on me completely.

After the funeral and when the estate began to be liquidated, it dawned on me that once all the assets were distributed, what would be the legacy left behind? What were the memories made and stories told that would be shared year after year with the kids, grandkids, and great-grandkids left behind? With his time on this earth, just like each of us, what would his legacy have been if he had put his focus on making a lasting difference in the Kingdom of God and focused on the two things that are eternal—people and the Word?

One thing I decided from having experienced that funeral was to make sure that none of my kids ask the pastor who presides over MY funeral, "What are you going to say about my dad?" Only God and a man can make that the answer we all want it to be!

Faking It

At the end of January 2018, something happened that I had never experienced before. I lost a close friend to suicide.

Everybody in town knew my friend and had great respect for his family. He was a very creative guy and owned his own marketing and design company. Even though, he would wind up using his creativity to help REUP mens movement, that wasn't how we had met.

He had drifted into my Sunday school class one morning by accident. He kept coming back and eventually we started spending some time together. He was hungry to learn and grow. He got involved with our REUP men's movement team, and he and I traveled to several states together doing men's events. He was a part of a Fire Team of guys that cared for and loved on each other.

My wife and I had set up a date that introduced him to the sweet woman he would wind up marrying. I actually had the honor of officiating their wedding.

But on a cold Tuesday evening in January, my phone rang and I saw it was his wife. When I answered, she was very emotional and hard to understand. I finally made out that she was saying her husband, my friend, was dead. I couldn't believe what she was saying but I hung up and my wife and I ran to my vehicle and headed directly to their home.

The local sheriff's department was a few minutes behind us. They immediately removed everyone from the scene and into the house. Most of the remainder of that evening was a whirlwind and I don't recall a lot of it. I was in shock.

The following day as everyone's heads started to clear and grasp the reality of what was happening, we started to try to piece together what had happened. He was one of the most joyful men I had ever been around. He was like a kid in a grownup's body. He loved everyone and was always the most positive guy to hang out with. He and I would go to football games together. Mylinda and I had gone on vacation with him and his wife. He loved life! WHY? I was so conflicted. Everybody was dumbfounded. What had happened? Why would he take his own life? WHY?

He was like a brother to me. I remember being outside of his home where a few friends were gathered the evening following his death. In my confusion and grief, I attacked the garbage dumpster in the driveway. I kicked and punched at it because I was so mad at him! Why didn't he come to me and let me help him?

Two days later, I officiated his funeral. The funeral home chapel was packed. I gave my best effort at honoring his life and tried to help everyone in attendance process what had happened. It was tough and painful but thank goodness the Lord took over and spoke through me.

As the days and weeks passed, we started to discover some ugly truths that were hidden beneath the surface of my friend's life. Unbeknownst to his wife he had gotten himself in some serious financial trouble, and the walls were tumbling down around him.

We ascertained that he wasn't the man we had seen on the outside. He was really faking it most of the time. He was under an extreme amount of pressure, yet he was masterful at hiding it. At some point he decided to take his life instead of facing reality and the truth. The enemy can deceive us into thinking that there is no way out, and that is what happened to my dear friend.

Here was a man who knew the truth, a man who had other men around him that knew the truth, a man who knew the value of men investing in other men and was doing it! Yet, it seems that he forgot about 1 Peter 5:8:

Be alert and of sober mind. Your enemy the devil prowls around like a roaring lion looking for someone to devour.[59]

This enemy never quits! He convinced my buddy to leave behind his wife, family, and friends and give up. You can only fake it for so long. This is serious. We are in a battle. My friend surrendered, and I will be forever heartbroken.

What No One Mentioned

In early 2019, I attended the funeral of another friend of mine who died unexpectedly. He had been a very successful attorney in my hometown of Murray. I knew him when I was a teenager prior to him having a life change very similar to what I had experienced. He had studied under Bob Warren as well and had been exposed to the same life changing truths that I had. The life changing identity truth that what we do is not who we are but who we are has a huge impact on what we do transformed my buddy. After the realization of this truth, I saw him live a life truly by the life of Another and watched God and an ordinary man make an impact on so many other people.

He started a Fire Team of men and assisted in helping numerous other teams get started. He gave away unknown amounts of money to individuals, non-profits, ministries, and schools. He helped start several organizations focused on assisting those in need. He went to elementary schools and read to kids. He was known as the Bubble Gum Guy, because he always had Double Bubble gum with him and gave it to kids.

He grew vegetables every summer and drove around town giving them away. He loved God's word. He loved to read and buy books to give away to others. He volunteered his time to be the Character Coach for local high school athletic teams because he believed the faith of the next generations was worth anything and everything. He went to Israel and The Holy Land a few times and taught classes on The Holy Land at churches around the region.

He would tell you that he used to be that guy that was trying to be successful at things that didn't matter, and he hurt lots of people along the way. Then he met Jesus and realized that God and a man could make a difference.

I attended his funeral on a cold and rainy day. I got to the funeral home early for the visitation, and I watched and listened to people talk about him and share stories with his son. I saw people from every walk of life show up to honor him. When the funeral service started, I scanned the room and saw a love and respect for this man unlike anything I had seen before. The two pastors told stories and shared scriptures that described my buddy.

As I was listening to the last pastor start to wrap up the service, something dawned on me. No one had mentioned anything about my buddy being an attorney. No one mentioned that he had done some amazing work on their legal actions. I am not exaggerating. It never got mentioned once. I almost raised my hand to ask if I could say something but decided not to.

WOW! What he did for a living never got mentioned, only what he had done for others and the difference he had made in their lives. He had been very successful as a lawyer, but once he decided to take his vocation and use it as a way to let Jesus live His life through him, he started to really live!

Which one of these guys are you?

- Side Road Sam, who encouraged everyone that has a voice to use that voice for the most important reason it's been given to them: to tell people about Jesus?

- Or my father-in-law, who wondered, "Oh my gosh, are they going to have anything good to say about me at my funeral?"
- Or, my dear friend, who recognized, "Nobody really knows what's going on inside me right now?"
- Or my buddy the attorney, who caused people to talk about his legacy and impact rather than his occupation?

I'm going to go with the kind of life Sam and my attorney buddy lived, a life where God and a man can do amazing things!

chapter fifteen

MANDEMIC

I have an old notebook where I jot down ideas as they have occurred to me. Twelve years ago, about the time I started REUP, I made an entry about what I called the "epidemic of indifference." I came across this entry recently, while writing this book in the middle of the COVID-19 pandemic that has occupied most of 2020. However, I believe we have been encountering a MANDEMIC for a good deal longer than that.

So, what is a "mandemic?" I touched on this a bit back in Chapter 7. Because men in our culture don't understand their identity in Christ, they sleepwalk through life without care or interest. They do not make emotional connections. They may show concern, but they rarely step up to do anything. Men today are apathetic, self-focused, and obsessed with worldly success and the material possessions, status, and lifestyle that accompany it.

Just as the COVID-19 virus is highly contagious and potentially devastating, so is a mandemic. No mask prevents it. It spreads quietly, evading notice. Then, one day you look up, and it's everywhere.

The worst part about a mandemic, though, is that it's teachable. Our sons watch their fathers and do what they do more than they will ever do what they say. Likewise, young men will also FAIL to do what their fathers don't, or won't, do. Author Steve Farrar put it this way in his book, *Standing Tall:*

> *I believe that when you look at every major pressing issue in this country, whether it's teenage pregnancy, child abuse, drive-by shootings, teenage suicides, or the divorce rate, and reduce each of these problems down to their lowest common denominator, you will find in each one the same root cause.*
> *That cause is a lack of male leadership.*[60]

So how did we find ourselves in this situation? As G. K. Chesterton wrote, "It isn't that they can't see the solution. It is that they can't see the problem."[61] The problem is that male leadership is all but invisible today. Men don't seem to be willing to invest in other men. They are not stepping up to lead by the example that Jesus set for us to follow. As masculinity is under attack, this is more critical than ever.

> *"The greatest crisis today is the crisis of leadership. And the greatest crisis of leadership is the crisis of character. We have to mentor character to others."*
>
> —Dr. Howard Hendricks

Why is it so important to build the next generations? Because one generation is all it takes to forget EVERYTHING we have learned. Remember back at the very beginning of this book when I recounted the story of Joshua being bold enough to ask God to make the sun stand still? Where did he get that boldness? I expect it had something to do with God telling him this to his face:

> *I will give you every place where you set your foot, as I promised Moses. Your territory will extend from the desert to Lebanon, and from the great river, the Euphrates—all the Hittite country—to the Mediterranean Sea in the west. No one will be able to stand against you all the days of your life. As I was with Moses, so I will be with you; I will never leave you nor forsake you. Be strong and courageous, because you will lead these people to inherit the land I swore to their ancestors to give them.*
>
> *"Be strong and very courageous. Be careful to obey all the law my servant Moses gave you; do not turn from it to the right or to the left, that you may be successful wherever you go. Keep this Book of the Law always on your lips; meditate on it day and night, so that you may be careful to do everything written in it. Then you will be prosperous and successful. Have I not commanded you? Be strong and courageous. Do not be afraid; do not be discouraged, for the LORD your God will be with you wherever you go."[62]*

What a confidence builder! Hearing straight from God that you are basically bulletproof? I would imagine that not just believing but KNOWING that God was with him gave Joshua all the drive he needed to lead the charge. God also gave Joshua instructions to do everything that Moses passed down to him. He needed to meditate on the word so that it would always lead him to success. Over and over, God reminds Joshua to be strong and to have courage, because God will always be with him.

This is how it's supposed to work. A generation passes its wisdom to the next generation so that the next generation can duplicate their successes and avoid their failures. That's how progress happens in any society, at least in theory. In reality, however, this happened:

*The people served the LORD **throughout the lifetime of Joshua and of the elders who outlived him and who had seen all the great things the LORD had done for Israel.***

*Joshua son of Nun, the servant of the LORD, died at the age of a hundred and ten. And they buried him in the land of his inheritance, at Timnath Heres **in the hill country of Ephraim, north of Mount** Gaash.*

*After that whole generation had been gathered to their ancestors, another generation grew up who knew neither the LORD **nor what he had done for Israel.** Then the Israelites did evil in the eyes of the LORD **and served the Baals.** They forsook the LORD, the God of their ancestors, who had brought them out of Egypt. They followed and worshiped various gods of the peoples around them. They aroused the LORD's anger because they forsook him and served Baal and the Ashtoreths. In his anger against Israel the LORD **gave them into the hands of raiders who plundered them.** He sold them into the hands of their enemies all around, whom they were no longer able to resist. Whenever Israel went out to fight, the hand of the LORD **was against them to defeat them, just as he had sworn to them.** They were in great distress.*

*Then the LORD **raised up judges, who saved them out of the hands of these raiders.** Yet they would not listen to their judges but prostituted themselves to other gods and worshiped them. They quickly turned from the ways of their ancestors, who had been obe-*

*dient to the LORD's commands. Whenever the LORD **raised up a** judge for them, he was with the judge and saved them out of the hands of their enemies as long as the judge lived; for the LORD **relented because of their groaning under those who oppressed and afflicted them. But when the judge died, the people returned to ways even more corrupt than those of their ancestors, following other gods and serving and worshiping them.** They refused to give up their evil practices and stubborn ways.*[63]

A single generation from the one that entered the promised land, and they have already forgotten God. Some of their grandparents had wandered through the desert following God's presence as a pillar of cloud by day and a pillar of fire by night. Didn't anybody tell that story to their kids? Did it not occur to any of them that passing down the commands God had given to Moses might be a good idea? Instead, they fell into idolatry, going along with the crowd of pagans that were not driven out of the promised land, because even Joshua, hero that he was, couldn't finish what he started. Down through the years, they repeated the pattern of only calling out to God when they were oppressed, but then turning back to their idols as soon as they got comfortable.

Does this sound familiar? It should because we are doing the same thing today. Our idol is the American Dream. American men are more concerned with making six figures than spending six nights a week with their families. Because of this, the American Dream has ruined our role as difference makers. Instead of being leaders, we have become slaves to our desire to have more stuff and to the debt that follows close behind. I wonder sometimes if we would be as enamored with stuff if we calculated the cost of it in time instead of money? Instead of saying, "That new Corvette will set me back about $65,000," what if we said instead, "That new Corvette will cost me three years of seventy-hour weeks?" Makes it a little less shiny, doesn't it? Especially when you consider that in gaining your sexy new car, you have lost touch with your kids and missed out on three years you could have been influencing them. To be a good dad, you don't have to be perfect; you just have to be present.

Money isn't the only false god in our lives though. Basically, an idol is anything that we place on the throne of our lives where God ought to be. Food is so easily obtained in our culture, it's very easy to make an idol out of food. How many men are "too busy" to go to church, but have plenty of time to golf or watch whatever sport is in season on Sunday? How many men "don't have time" to study their Bible, but spend hours a night in front of Netflix or scrolling through social media?

And what about sex? Most of us church-going menfolk wouldn't like to admit that sex could be an idol in our lives, but the statistics tell a different story. The porn industry currently has a net worth of $97 billion dollars. That's more than Major League Baseball, the NFL and the NBA combined. Porn sites get more visitors than Netflix, Amazon and Twitter combined. Mind Geek, which owns four major porn sites, is the third largest bandwidth-consuming company in the world, trailing only Netflix and Google.[64]

In a mandemic, men have lost their way, because they are confused about their roles and their influence. Men just don't know who they are as men. As a result, boys grow up not knowing how to become men. Dennis Prager wrote on this topic in his article, "Is America Still Making Men?" back in 2010:

> When I acted immaturely, I was told to be or act like a man. I wonder how many boys are told to "be a man" today; and if they were, would they have a clue as to what that meant? It would appear that for millions of American boys, this has not been the reality for decades. Many families and society as a whole seem to have forgotten boys need to be made into men.
>
> When boys do not become men, women assume their roles. But they are not happy doing so. There are any number of reasons American women suffer from depression more than ever before and more than men. It is difficult to believe that one of those reasons is not the very emasculation of men that the movement working in their name helped to bring about. And so, a vicious cycle has commenced -- men stop being men; women become man-like; men retreat even further from their manly role; and women get sadder.[65]

Meanwhile, the side effects of this mandemic are unavoidable. The divorce rate is increasing. Fatherless homes are at an all-time high. Consumer debt is at a record amount. Instead of handling and finding solutions for these significant problems, men are retreating to their "man caves" to find their escape in video games and fantasy sports leagues. They don't have manly friendships, they don't take any risks, and they are not hungry for a cause.

As a result, young women today aren't wanting to be married to these young men. Men are stepping away from their traditional roles of leading their homes and families. Since men have abdicated their role as leaders, women are stepping up out of necessity. More women are leading companies than ever before. Many of them are doing a great job, of course, but that doesn't address the issue that women cannot be fathers.

So, instead of the family being a training ground for the next generation of leaders, we have kids killing kids in school and on the streets. Young men are rioting in cities across America, because they have no idea how to deal with adversity and pain in a healthy way. Islam is growing at a rapid rate with young men because it is focused on being "manly." And do I even need to mention the gender identity confusion that is plaguing this generation?

People born between 1983 and 2000 are known as the Millennial Generation. When asked if they were "born-again Christians," only 20% of millennials affirmed the definition of belief and experience. When presented with seven statements of orthodox Christian belief, only 6% could affirm them and thus be properly defined as Evangelicals. An unreached people group is defined as "any ethnic or ethno-linguistic group without enough Christians to evangelize the rest of the nation. A 5% population is necessary threshold to accomplish this goal." Between the publication of *The Millennial* in 2011 and the end of 2012, that 6% dropped to 4.25%. So, the millennial generation is now considered an unreached people group, right now and right here in America! That's sad, but this is sadder—we are the generation that let this happen.

Now for some good news. There is a cure for this mandemic, and the cure is also contagious and teachable. We need to stop letting our buddies off the hook by accepting their excuses. When they say, "I'll get to it later," instead of going back to our band of brothers and saying, "Well, he's really busy right now," we need to develop and express a sense of urgency about the seriousness of this mandemic.

If we are to reverse the trend of men failing to pass on wisdom to future generations, then our generation needs to remind itself of what we learned. What has God done in our lives, and what does He require of His followers? One of the last things that Joshua did, after Israel had entered the promised land, was to renew Israel's covenant with God by reminding them how they got where they were, and by issuing this challenge:

Joshua said to all the people, "This is what the LORD, the God of Israel, says: 'Long ago your ancestors, including Terah the father of Abraham and Nahor, lived beyond the Euphrates River and worshiped other gods. But I took your father Abraham from the land beyond the Euphrates and led him throughout Canaan and gave him many descendants. I gave him Isaac, and to Isaac I gave Jacob and Esau. I assigned the hill country of Seir to Esau, but Jacob and his family went down to Egypt.

"'Then I sent Moses and Aaron, and I afflicted the Egyptians by what I did there, and I brought you out. When I brought your people out of Egypt, you came to the sea, and the Egyptians pursued them with chariots and horsemen as far as the Red Sea. But they cried to the LORD for help, and he put darkness between you and the Egyptians; he brought the sea over them and covered them. You saw with your own eyes what I did to the Egyptians. Then you lived in the wilderness for a long time.

"'I brought you to the land of the Amorites who lived east of the Jordan. They fought against you, but I gave them into your hands. I destroyed them from before you, and you took possession of their land. When Balak son of Zippor, the king of Moab, prepared to fight against Israel, he sent for Balaam son of Beor to put a curse on you. But I would not listen to Balaam, so he blessed you again and again, and I delivered you out of his hand.

"'Then you crossed the Jordan and came to Jericho. The citizens of Jericho fought against you, as did also the Amorites, Perizzites, Canaanites, Hittites, Girgashites, Hivites and Jebusites, but I gave them into your hands. I sent the hornet ahead of you, which drove them out before you—also the two Amorite kings.

141

You did not do it with your own sword and bow. So I gave you a land on which you did not toil and cities you did not build; and you live in them and eat from vineyards and olive groves that you did not plant.'

"Now fear the LORD and serve him with all faithfulness. Throw away the gods your ancestors worshiped beyond the Euphrates River and in Egypt, and serve the LORD. But if serving the LORD seems undesirable to you, then choose for yourselves this day whom you will serve, whether the gods your ancestors served beyond the Euphrates, or the gods of the Amorites, in whose land you are living. But as for me and my household, we will serve the LORD."[66]

If we take an honest look back at our lives, I am certain that we can all find things that the Lord has delivered us from. I have just spent the last fourteen chapters telling you about some of mine. We didn't earn the forgiveness God offers us in Christ, but He extended it to us anyway, first because He wanted to, and second because He alone has the authority to. That should be more than sufficient for us to have a reverent fear of the Lord and throw off everything in our lives that hinders us from serving Him.

To do this, we must be willing to lose or give up something to let God use us for His glory and purposes. Maybe, we give up a few of our hobbies (golf, hunting, etc.) for a season or two and find ways to invest in young men. Maybe we let go of our worldly desires and focus on emptying what's in our "buckets" into another man's bucket. If 2020 has shown us anything, it is that we need to be prepared to be disliked, discredited, and even disowned by the world's system, because it will probably happen. Therefore, we need to have the courage to stand firm and be MEN! And with this courage, we must add contentment, following Paul's example:

I know how to live when I am poor and when I have plenty. I have learned the secret of how to live through any kind of situation—when I have enough to eat or when I am hungry, when I have everything I need or when I have nothing. Christ is the one who gives me the strength I need to do whatever I must do.[67]

chapter sixteen

TODAY IS THE DAY, AND NOW IS THE TIME

I am an old football player, and for that reason, I have an intense mentality about things. One of my common sayings is, "Let's don't talk about blocking and tackling. Let's actually block and tackle." In other words, talking accomplishes nothing. Let's take action. Men are naturally wired this way. We want to see progress. We want to see results. As Larry the Cable Guy would say, we want to "Git 'er done!"

"Nobody ever got ready by waiting. You only get ready by starting."[68]

Let's start then. It's time to make some changes and start pursuing God's heart and our true identity in Christ. It's time to start living by His life in us.

Therefore, since we have been justified by faith, we have peace with God through our Lord Jesus Christ.[69]

What does it mean to be justified? Holman's Bible Dictionary defines justification as the "process by which an individual is brought into an unmerited relationship with God."[70] I have also heard it defined as "Just as if I never sinned before." Either or both apply to what happened to me in an instant of time when I realized my need for a Savior, repented of my sins, and asked Jesus into my life.

Wow! I was no longer in a state of condemnation (Romans 8:1). I was made righteous, meaning "right with God," (1 Corinthians 1:30), and it was all done by one thing – faith in Christ (Galatians 3:16). It wasn't done by me cleaning up my act or asking Him into my life, then going to work to earn my justification.

In Romans 5:1, the word justified is in the past tense, which means it is a completed action. If you have put your trust in Christ, then you and I have become saints, holy people set apart for God's purposes, no matter what we have done in the past! Paul confirms we are saints in 1 Corinthians 1:2. We are not perfect in our behavior; thus, we are saints who occasionally sin. God granted us repentance (2 Timothy 2:25 and Acts 11:18), gave us faith (Romans 12:3), and then justified us. That which is true of Christ is now true of all believers, because we are in Christ! It's time we started living in the past tense of what Jesus died for us to be—justified!

The following table lists just a few verses that confirm who we really are in Christ. They illustrate scriptural traits that reflect whom you would become in just a moment's time. You don't have to earn them. You can't buy them. You ARE them through our Lord Jesus Christ.

Hebrews 10:14	*Perfected*
Galatians 2:20	*Crucified with Christ*
Colossians 3:3	*Hidden with Christ*
1 Corinthians 1:2	*Saint*
Romans 8:30	*Justified, Glorified*
Philippians 3:20	*Citizen of Heaven*
1 Peter 5:8	*Enemy of the Devil*
2 Corinthians 5:21	*Righteousness of God*
1 Corinthians 1:30	*In Christ Jesus*
Ephesians 1:4	*Holy and Blameless*
Romans 6:6	*A Slave to Sin no Longer*
Colossians 3:13	*Forgiven*
Romans 8:1	*Not Condemned*
Romans 5:9	*Safe from God's Wrath*
2 Corinthians 5:17	*New Creation*

Those who are "in Christ" are those who have faith in Him, and their sin is forgiven by Christ's death in their place. Those in Christ are new creatures. Their identity has changed from being the fallen version of themselves, to being associated with the righteousness of Christ.

These are all completed actions. Past tense. We won't become them someday. We are them now in God's eyes, even though our behavior and actions will vary each day. We are not on a performance-based deal with Him. We live under His grace. When Jesus said on the cross, "It is finished," this is what He was talking about. To learn more about this, I highly recommend that you work through *IDENTITY: Who I Am In Christ* offered through REUP Men's Movement.

Because of this, we all have the foundation in place to become men of God. You are God's man! However, even though we don't earn our standing with God, we do have some business to take care of in our lives down here on earth. We must learn from the past and not let it define us. We must embrace the fact that He lives IN us and then let Him live His life THROUGH us. We must learn to embrace pain as an opportunity. We have to step into uncomfortable. We must ask God to break our hearts for what breaks His. Most of all, we must always remember that the men we are someday going to be, we are NOW becoming!

Our days are numbered, and we don't know what the number is. One thing we do know, however, is that whatever tomorrow is going to look like will be decided by what we do today.

One night, at a men's event at a local church, I had spoken to about 500 men. It was a very impactful night. A bunch of men made some bold decisions and a bunch more stepped into the REUP context and joined Fire Teams. My dad was in town for the event and spent the night with us. Before I went to bed that night, my dad and I were talking in my living room. He's not known for being a touchy, huggy kind of guy, but he reached over, grabbed me, and pulled me in close to him. Then he started to cry, and he said something that will be forever etched in my mind.

He said, "I just want you to know that what I saw you do tonight up in front of all those men, and how God's using you right now to impact men—I just want to tell you as your dad, that's what you were created to do. I have no doubt in my mind. That's what you were created to do." Then he hugged me real hard. I turned and went down the hallway, and I just lost it. It was such a validation. For him to say to me that of all the things I've done in my life, what I was made to do was to speak truth, challenge and encourage men, and invest all my energy into to helping them become the difference makers that THEY were created to be. It pierced my heart. I'm convinced it was my Heavenly Father using my earthly father to encourage me to keep giving my life away for the sake of others and for Him!

What's interesting to me is that every other man was made to do the same thing. Your Heavenly Father, like my earthly father, is saying to you that you were made to be God's man and that you should do everything in your power to live that out for the rest of your days. Despite your struggles and mistakes, you are God's man. The enemy is constantly trying to get you to believe otherwise. God made you in His image and to specifically do something. Could it be to "pick a fight?" Let me explain.

I've read Bob Goff's book *Love Does* twice. I'm not sure I have ever read any book twice. In this book, Goff tells the story about a childhood bully. The boy was a good-sized seventh grader named Dale who bullied the smaller sized boys in his school. Goff shares that he was a big kid himself, and one day he saw Dale beat up another kid, a little kid. Goff proceeded to challenge Dale to a fistfight.

They scheduled the fight for the following day. By the time a teacher stepped into break up the fight, "Dale was covered in blood. Nobody realized it was all mine..."[71] Goff had taken up the cause for somebody else and had laid it on the line.

What's the point of me telling you this story? I think the idea of picking a fight on behalf of others is a guiding insight as to what is happening with men today. I think it is a clue as to why we have become so passive instead of picking a fight. It's one thing to defend ourselves when we get attacked. It's another to go pick a fight on behalf of someone or something. Could it be that we need to pick a fight for the next generations? Until we pick a fight, we won't know what we're made of. Or made for.

Do you realize that a purpose is all about the WHY? We know that God created each of us for a purpose and that purpose centers around other people. Author Jon Acuff says that purpose is a simple formula:

Your talent + other people = Purpose

I would add something to this formula:

**Your talent + Your willingness to change +
Your pursuit of God's heart + Other People = Purpose**

In his devotion, *Radical Wisdom*, Regi Campbell says the following...

> A fight musters resources. A fight pumps adrenaline. A fight creates urgency. A big fight forces you to look outside yourself and create alliances. In a fight, there are times you attack and times you protect. A fight keeps you focused on your adversary.
>
> Don't leave God out of this—He's given you talents and experiences like no one else. Ask Him to make it clear by giving you a burden for the fight He wants you to pick. Ask Him to wear you out until you act.[72]

What Jesus would have us do is often different from what we want to do. What He wants us to do will be costly, risky, and even difficult at times. What's cool about that is it sounds manly and it sounds like an adventure. A good old-fashioned fight has that John Wayne imagery. It's time to pick your fight. Today is the day and now is the time!

We must learn to embrace pain as an opportunity. We have to step into uncomfortable. We must ask God to break our hearts for what breaks His.

You've heard my story. You've seen the way forward. You know your days are numbered. Now it's time to let God prove to you that He is who He says He is. God can use any man to make a difference, if that man will decide to pursue God's heart, because God IS who He says He is!

I have come to the realization that people and God's word are the only two things that are eternal. Every person will live eternally somewhere, it's just a matter of where. God's word will always be. Therefore, I have decided to invest the rest of my time on earth to these two things. Everything else is really an exercise in futility.

Your life is passing you by like a hand waving from the back of a train, and every choice determines whether you are on the right track. It all matters.

"For the eyes of the Lord range throughout the earth to strengthen those whose hearts are fully committed to him."[73]

Then I heard the voice of the Lord saying, "Whom shall I send? And who will go for us?"
And I said, "Here am I. Send me!"[74]

Are you that man? I believe you are! Now, let's get busy picking our fight. Let's lock our arms with our Creator. Let's give Him the chance to prove that God and a man can truly make a difference. Today is the day. Now is the time. You are the man.

NOTES

1   Joshua 10:7-14 *Holy Bible, New International Version®*, NIV®
    Copyright © 1973, 1978, 1984, 2011 by Biblica, Inc.® (NIV)
2   Eames, C. (March 2019). *Thetrumpet.com.* (Philadelphia
    Church of God, 2020) Retrieved April 3, 2020, from *https://
    www.thetrumpet.com/18558-and-the-sun-stood-still*
3   James 5:17 (NIV)
4   1 Kings 18:36-39 (NIV)
5   Genesis 41: 46-49, 53-57 *New American Standard Bible,
    NASB Copyright* © 1960, 1962, 1963, 1968, 1971, 1972,
    1973, 1975, 1977, 1995 by the Lockman Foundation (NASB)
6   1 Samuel 17:50b-54 *The Holy Bible, English Standard Version*
    Copyright © 2001 by Crossway Bibles, a publishing ministry
    of Good News Publishers. (ESV)
7   2 Chronicles 16:9a (NIV)
8   1 Samuel 16:7 (NIV)
9   2 Chronicles 16:9 Amplified Bible Copyright © 2015 by
    The Lockman Foundation, La Habra, CA 90631. All Rights
    Reserved. (AMP)
10 (ESV)
11 *Ibid*
12 (NIV)
13 Psalm 51:3-6, 10-15 (NIV)
14 Luke 15:15-16 (NASB)
15 Romans 5:10 (NASB)
16 2 Timothy 2:2 (NASB)
17 Ludy, Eric (2008) *The Brave Hearted Gospel*. Eugene, OR:
    Harvest House Publishers. Retrieved from https://www.
    google.com/books/edition/The_Bravehearted_Gospel/O7Xdz
    YET0BMC?hl=en&gbpv=1&printsec=frontcover
18 www.livingbyhislife.com

19 https://www.livingbyhislife.com/about/the-numbers/
20 Romans 5:2b-5 (NASB)
21 Revelation 2:4 (NASB)
22 Brown, Tim. (2020, February 12). *Leading as a Jesus Guy...*
Part 2 with Jess Correll [Audio podcast]. Retrieved from
https://anchor.fm/tim-brown4/
23 *Common English Bible* Copyright © 2011 by Common
English Bible (CEB)
24 *Ibid*
25 2 Corinthians 5:17 The Holy Bible, Evangelical Heritage
Version®, EHV®, © 2019 Wartburg Project, Inc. All rights
reserved. (EHV)
26 2 Corinthians 5:14-20 *Holy Bible. New Living Translation*
copyright© 1996, 2004, 2007 by Tyndale House Foundation.
Used by permission of Tyndale House Publishers Inc., Carol
Stream, Illinois 60188. All rights reserved. (NLT)
27 2 Chronicles 16:9a (AMP)
28 (ESV)
29 (NIV)
30 2 Chronicles 15:2b (NIV)
31 2 Chronicles 16:7-8 (NASB)
32 2 Chronicles 16:9a (NASB)
33 John 17:24 (NASB)
34 Psalm 24:1a New International Reader's Version Copyright ©
1995, 1996, 1998, 2014 by Biblica, Inc.®. Used by permission.
All rights reserved worldwide. (NIRV)
35 (NIV)
36 Matthew 6:19-21 (NIV)
37 Giglio, Louie. (2006). *Wired for a Life of Worship.* Retrieved
from http://worship.com/2007/03/louie-giglio-wired-for-a-
life-of-worship-part-1/
38 Philippians 2:5-8 (NASB)
39 Romans 9: 1-3 (NASB)
40 John 10:10 New Revised Standard Version (NRSV) New
Revised Standard Version Bible, copyright © 1989 the
Division of Christian Education of the National Council of
the Churches of Christ in the United States of America. Used
by permission. All rights reserved.

41 Romans 12:2 (NASB)
42 Nehemiah 1:1-3 (NASB)
43 The Passion Translation The Passion Translation®. Copyright © 2017 by BroadStreet Publishing® Group, LLC. Used by permission. All rights reserved. thePassionTranslation.com (TPT)
44 Nehemiah 1:4 (NASB)
45 Nehemiah 1:4-11a (NASB)
46 Ecclesiastes 1:9 (NASB)
47 (NASB)
48 Hebrews 11:6 (NASB)
49 1 Kings 19:19-21 (NLT)
50 Ezekiel 22:30 (NASB)
51 1 John 1:1-4 (NASB)
52 James 1:22 (NASB)
53 Luke 19:8 (NASB)
54 Matthew 28:18-20 (NASB)
55 (ESV)
56 Job 14:5 New Life Version Copyright © 1969, 2003 by Barbour Publishing, Inc. (NLV)
57 Psalm 90:12 (NLV)
58 (NLT)
59 (NIV)
60 Farrar, Steve (2011) *Standing Tall: How a Man Can Protect His Family.* Crown Publishing Group
61 Chesterton, G.K. (1935) *The Scandal of Father Brown.* G. K. Hall & Company.
62 Joshua 1: 3-9 (NIV)
63 Judges 2:7-19 (NIV)
64 *How Big is the Porn Industry?* Medium.com. Retrieved August 12, 2020 from https://medium.com/@TheSBT/how-big-is-the-porn-industry-fbc1ac78091b
65 Prager, Dennis. (January 19, 2010) *Is America Still Making Men?* The Dennis Prager Show.
66 Joshua 24:2-15 (NIV)
67 Philippians 4:12-13 Easy-to-Read Version Copyright © 2006 by Bible League International (ERV)
68 Maxwell, John C. (2012) *The 15 Invaluable Laws of Growth: Live Them and Reach Your Potential* Center Street

69 Romans 5:1 Modern English Version The Holy Bible,
    Modern English Version. Copyright © 2014 by Military
    Bible Association. Published and distributed by Charisma
    House. (MEV)

70 Butler, Trent C. Editor. Entry for 'Justification'. Holman
    Bible Dictionary. https://www.studylight.org/dictionaries/
    hbd/j/justification.html. 1991.

71 Goff, Bob (2012) *Love Does* Thomas Nelson

72 Campbell, Regi (2018) *Radical Wisdom* iDisciple Publishing

73 2 Chronicles 16:9a (NIV)

74 Isaiah 6:8 (NIV)

REUP was founded in 2009 as a means to build men into the difference makers they were created to be. We have seen a large number of men from various states utilize the structures and resources we provide to move them closer to Jesus and assist in helping them live by HIS life.

Now it is time to go further faster as we see the next generations struggle and lose hope that our world could be different. We need a movement of God in our country and REUP believes that the starting point is a movement of men.

REUP is not a ministry or a program. It is a movement of men. It is a disciple making system that truly educates, encourages, and empowers men. Our goal is to create a national movement across communities, churches and companies.

REUP is a personal adventure into intimacy with Jesus Christ, rather than a program about getting men involved in the church.

We believe our primary objective is to lead men to the feet of Christ—not simply into a small group or some short study about Him. We do this by creating intentional structures with constant encouragement and focus.

EDUCATE men in the Father, ENCOURAGE them as they pursue the Father, EMPOWER them as they grow in the Father alongside other men; and you create a culture of expectation and accountability that gives you a foundation for a true disciple-making in your church or company!

www.livingbyhislife.com
https://www.facebook.com/livingbyhislife
https://twitter.com/TimReup
https://www.instgram.com/timreup/

ABOUT THE AUTHOR

For Tim Brown's entire life, God has placed him in positions that surrounded him with men. From childhood athletics, clerking in a men's store during the high school and college years, owning his own men's clothing store, to working for a national custom clothing maker — Tim has spent each day speaking one-on-one with men in our society.

Tim has written a number of Bible studies that have been utilized by men to help them discover their identity in Christ and how to live in that truth.

Tim has a passion to know God's heart and to help others learn to live by Christ's life in them. Tim started *FHG Clothiers* and founded *REUP Men's Movement* that has been utilized by thousands of men and also is the founding pastor of *Church @ The Corner* in his community of Bowling Green, Ky.

He has been married to his wife Mylinda for over thirty-five years, is the father of two sons, and is "Poppa" to three grandkids.

SCRIPTURAL REFERENCES

Scripture references appear bold, page numbers appear italic.

OLD TESTAMENT

Genesis
37:3, 40:5-19, 41:1-32 • *pp 15*

Exodus
3:11 • *pp 79;* 4:10 • *pp 79;* 17:13 • *pp 12*

Numbers
13:8, 16 • *pp 12*

Deuteronomy
1:38, 31:3, 7-8, 34:9 • *pp 12*

Joshua
1, 6:2-27 • *pp 12*

2 Samuel
11:1 • *pp 100*

1 Kings
17:4-6 • *pp 14;* 19 • *pp 111;* 9:21 • *pp 112*

2 Chronicles
14:11 • *pp 93;* 16:7 • *pp 94*

Nehemiah
2:1-5 • *pp 109*

Psalm
1 • *pp 100;* 24 • *pp 97;* 37:4 • *pp 88;* 90:12 • *pp 100*

Proverbs
11:14, 11:24, 13:10, 15:31, 19:17, 22:9, 27:20, 30:7-9 • *pp 101;* 22:7 • *pp 100*

Ecclesiastes
2:4-11 • *pp 100*

NEW TESTAMENT

Matthew
24:12 • *pp 104*

Mark
8:36 • *pp 39;* 16:20 • *pp 120*

Luke
10:27-28 • *pp 128;* 18 • *pp 117;* 19 • *pp 117*

John
3:16 • *pp 63;* 8:32 • *pp 53, 125;* 10:10 • *pp 85;* 15:5 • *pp 18*

Acts
11:18 • *pp 144*

Romans
1:21-22; 25 • *pp 41;* 5:1, 5:9, 6:6, 12:3 • *pp 144;* 8:1 • *pp 143, 144;* 8:30 • *pp 101, 144*

1 Corinthians
1:2 • *pp 144;* 1:30 • *pp 143, 144;* 2:2 • *pp 90*

2 Corinthians
5:17 • *pp 144;* 5:21 • *pp 101, 144;* 9:6 • *pp 101*

Galatians
2:20 • *pp 144;* 3:16 • *pp 143*

Ephesians
1:4 • *pp 144;* 5:16 • *pp 100*

Philippians
1:21 • *pp 128;* 3:10 • *pp 101;* 3:20 • *pp 144*

Colossians
3:1-4 • *pp 97;* 3:3, 3:13 • *pp 144;* 3:21 • *pp 100*

1 Timothy
4:8 • *pp 100*

2 Timothy
2:25 • *pp 144*

Hebrews
4:9 • *pp 61;* 10:14 • *pp 144;* 12:2 • *pp 93*

1 Peter
5:8 • *pp 40, 132, 144*

Revelation
2:4 • *pp 77, 78*

INDEX

Louisville, Kentucky 75
Love Does 146
Ludy, Eric 67
Luther, Martin 108

M

Majors, Katie Davis 118
MD Anderson Cancer Center
75
Morehead State University
31, 32
Murray, Kentucky 25, 50, 52,
61, 65, 83, 88, 89
Murray State University 29
My Utmost for His Highest 77

N

Norton's Hospital 75

P

Paducah, Kentucky 35, 89
Paine, Thomas 108
Paris, Tennessee 127
Prager, Dennis 139

R

Radical Wisdom 147
REUP 71, 72, 80, 81, 117,
125, 127, 131, 145, 153
Rimmer, Harry 13

S

Somerset, Kentucky 38, 48
Standing Tall 135
Stanford, Kentucky 65
Story, Harvey 6

T

The Hill 8, 60
Tom James Clothing Com-
pany 51, 55, 56, 73, 81
Trumpet, The 13

U

University of Mississippi 29,
31

V

Vanderbilt University Hospital
76

W

Warren, Bob 6, 9, 10, 28, 29,
43, 54, 60, 61, 63, 64, 66,
67, 70, 74, 78, 86, 89, 101,
132
Warren, Glenn 69
Webb, Jack 12

See More Great Books

at

WWW.ACCLAIMPRESS.COM

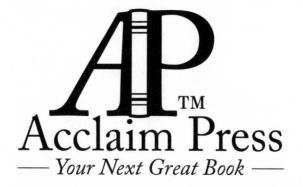